SAINTS

SAINTS

ANCIENT&MODERN

Barbara Calamari & Sandra DiPasqua

Viking Studio

We dedicate this book to the kids:
Emma, Paolo, Nicole, and Raymond.

VIKING STUDIO
Published by the Penguin Group
Penguin Group (USA) Inc., 375 Hudson Street, New York, New York 10014, U.S.A.
Penguin Group (Canada), 90 Eglinton Avenue East, Suite 700, Toronto, Ontario,
Canada M4P 2Y3 (a division of Pearson Penguin Canada Inc.)   ·   Penguin Books Ltd,
80 Strand, London WC2R 0RL, England   ·   Penguin Ireland, 25 St. Stephen's Green,
Dublin 2, Ireland (a division of Penguin Books Ltd)   ·   Penguin Books Australia Ltd,
250 Camberwell Road, Camberwell, Victoria 3124, Australia (a division of Pearson
Australia Group Pty Ltd)   ·   Penguin Books India Pvt Ltd, 11 Community Centre,
Panchsheel Park, New Delhi – 110 017, India   ·   Penguin Group (NZ), Cnr Airborne
and Rosedale Roads, Albany, Auckland 1310, New Zealand (a division of Pearson New
Zealand Ltd)   ·   Penguin Books (South Africa) (Pty) Ltd, 24 Sturdee Avenue, Rosebank,
Johannesburg 2196, South Africa

Penguin Books Ltd, Registered Offices: 80 Strand, London WC2R 0RL, England

First published in 2007 by Viking Studio,
a member of Penguin Group (USA) Inc.

1   3   5   7   9   10   8   6   4   2

Copyright © Barbara Calamari and Sandra Di Pasqua, 2007
All rights reserved

Illustration credits appear on page 150.

ISBN 978-0-670-03849-7

Printed in China
Set in Adobe Garamond
Designed by Sandra Di Pasqua

✠

ACKNOWLEDGMENTS

We must extend our gratitude to a host of people who have not only made this book possible, but who also did a great deal to improve it. First, we are indebted to the staff of Viking Studio and its publisher, Megan Newman, for providing us a wonderful working atmosphere. Amy Hill, the design director, Spring Hoteling in the design department, and Grace Veras, production manager, allowed us complete freedom of design while offering expert technical advice. Dara Stewart, our editor, saw to it that we were put in the talented hands of Rebecca Behan, who is not only an excellent editor herself, but also did much to shepherd this project through the production process.

Shirley Santino is owed a great deal of thanks for her much needed assistance in finding a voice and structure for the manuscript. Deborah Rust has been with us on every project, providing technical assistance; her help is invaluable to us. We are fortunate to have access to the work of photographers Lisa Silvestri, Robert Forlini, Larry Racioppo, and David McDonald. Father Eugene Carrella can provide an exquisite picture of any saint on a moment's notice and we are grateful for his generosity in working with us. Many of our beautiful images are edited paintings from the extensive collection of Art Resources in New York City, which has been most cooperative and helpful, and working with Linda Lee and its knowledgeable staff is always a pleasure. Finally, we must thank our agent, Jim Fitzgerald, as well as Brother Michael La Mantia of Our Lady of Pompeii Church, Patricia Bates, and Louis Turchioe for their steady support.

v

CONTENTS

INTRODUCTION

Catholics love the saints. They look upon them as protectors, family members, and living examples of how an ordinary life can experience an extraordinary transformation. Since no one is born a saint, these holy people have made terrible mistakes with which we can all identify. There are murderers, gamblers, and alcoholics among their numbers. They have suffered unimaginable cruelties and conquered every problem in the human condition, from bad marriages to fatal illnesses. Many who lived dissolutely and scandalously before their conversion were rewarded with ridicule and persecution for turning their backs on conventional society. In emulation of Christ, they refused to compromise their spiritual beliefs to preserve their worldly comforts. Through it all they emerge triumphant, willing to help those on earth find God by praying for us and with us.

For more than two thousand years, the legends and stories of the Christian saints have greatly affected the course of Western civilization. The saints have influenced our holidays, our school systems, the boundaries of nations, our poetry, music, and visual arts. They have been great philosophers, uneducated savants, mystics, administrators, farmers, housewives, and soldiers, hailing from every social strata of society.

The stories of the ancient saints seem more like legends to us today and, indeed, these tales once served as the only form of popular entertainment. As a result, the exploits of these holy people became more grandiose and exaggerated upon each telling. Thousands of years ago there were few written accounts of saints' lives. Most of their stories were told visually by painters, sculptors, and stained-glass artists who concentrated on the most imaginative and fantastic aspects of their biographies. For this reason a majority of saints are depicted with the power to overturn all natural laws. Saint Lucy calmly holds her eyeballs on a dish, Saint Nicholas raises three boys from the dead, and Saint Ursula is shot with arrows as she shields young girls under her cloak.

This haunting and dreamy iconography carried over in the depiction of modern saints as well. Visual portraits of the saints attempted to relay their stories with attributes or symbols contained in a single image. Saint Francis is often shown talking to animals or receiving the stigmata, Thérèse of Lisieux showers the viewer with roses, and Saint Anthony's kindness is symbolized by the image of the Christ child, who sits in his arms. These visual portrayals of the saints are vital reminders of their earthly existence. One sees them everywhere, in private homes, in churches, on clothing and jewelry, and even on the exterior walls of buildings.

Every town and country has saints that are familiar to the local residents and obscure to the rest of us. Since it is estimated that there are more than ten thousand formally recognized saints, it was possible to profile only a very few for this book. Instead of brief biographies and images of many significant saints, we opted to go into detail about a varied handful that have an ongoing influence in modern life. The saints we have chosen are in no way the most important or exalted; many are extremely popular, some less well known. They bring with them a mix of personalities and ethnic cultures that reflect the makeup of today's diverse society.

For this book, we have divided the first two thousand years of Christianity into ancient and modern time periods. The ancient saints span from prehistory to the year A.D. 1000. These saints tend to have more legendary aspects to their stories, resulting from the strong oral tradition in which they thrived. However, the modern saints are well documented by contemporary historical texts. These comprise the second thousand years. Some of these saints have influenced whole nations while others, through their particular state of life, encourage us to have a more personal relationship with them.

Statue of Saint Anne with Mary

✢

Introduction

saints

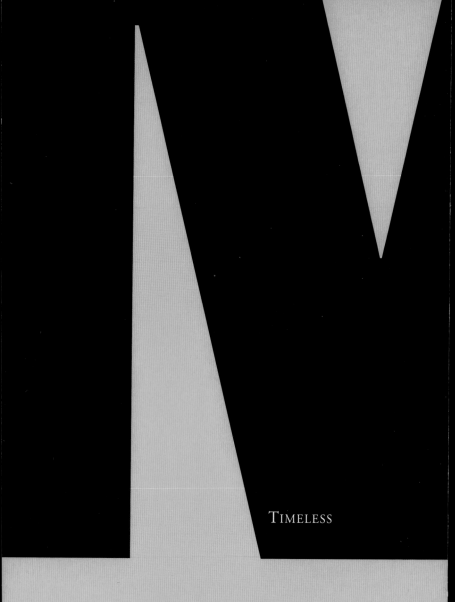

TIMELESS

Saint Michael
The Archangel

Feast Day: September 29
Patron of: Belgium, Brussels, England, Germany, Umbria,
firemen, grocers, health, knights, mariners, policemen, soldiers
Invoked for: good health, a holy death, physical protection
Symbols: defeating the devil or a serpent, scales, sword

Saint Michael predates the Christian religion and all other saints. Considered the most powerful being in the hierarchy of angels, he is honored in the Muslim and Jewish faiths as much as he is in Catholicism. Though he has never had a human existence, Saint Michael is closely tied to the fate of mankind and has been its guardian, defending good over evil, since the beginning of time. When the end of the world draws near, he will make his presence known by defeating the Antichrist. As foretold in the Book of Daniel [12:1], "And at that time shall Michael stand up, the great prince which standeth for the children of thy people: and there shall be a time of trouble, such as never was since there was a nation *even* to that same time." After he casts the Antichrist into hell, he will sound the trumpet calling for the Eternal Judgment, where the dead will receive their final reward or punishment.

As written in the Book of Revelation, Lucifer was the most beautiful and favored of God's angels. However, he became prideful and he decided that he was God's equal. A battle broke out in heaven between Lucifer and an angel who was heaven's protector. As the battle raged, those loyal to God cried out, "Mi-cha-el?" (Hebrew for, "Who is like God?"). Lucifer and his followers were defeated and cast into hell for their vanity. The Archangel who had led the charge to protect heaven took the name Michael.

Despite rabbinical warnings against appealing to anyone but God, the ancient Jews saw Michael as an intermediary devoted to their protection, as he had defended God against Lucifer. From its earliest days, Church elders have looked to Michael as the protector of Christianity as well. From scriptural passages in both old and new testaments, Michael has four mandates: 1) to fight against Lucifer; 2) to rescue the souls of the faithful from the power of the enemy, especially at the hour of death; 3) to be the champion of God's

✠

Saint Michael

people and protector of the Church; and 4) to bring souls to judgment.

Catholics believe Saint Michael and the Virgin Mary are the only beings besides Jesus able to descend into hell and release the souls suffering there. Because he vanquished Lucifer in heaven, the fallen angel has no power over Michael, even in his own domain. Since Lucifer dwells in the lowest, darkest region, then Michael, his opposite, must inhabit those points closest to heaven.

For this reason, shrines to Saint Michael are always on the highest, most inaccessible cliffs that only a celestial being capable of flight could reach. In ancient times they were visible from great distances but nearly impossible to approach, increasing their mystical appeal. One such sanctuary, founded in the dark ages is Skellig Michael, a fantastic natural monument. Dedicated to the archangel, Celtic monks built a monastery on the steep, rocky island eight miles from Kerry, Ireland, in 588. Escaping the chaos of warring tribes on the mainland, they created an ascetic environment to bring them nearer to God. Monks inhabited this shrine, living in the harshest conditions for over six hundred years. Because of its severe isolation and the impossibility of hosting visitors, Skellig Michael stands as one of the most well-preserved holy sites in the world.

Another famous yet inhospitable site dedicated to Saint Michael is the Gargano cave system in Apulia, Italy. Said to be a dwelling place for the archangel, it was miraculously discovered in the year 490 by a wealthy army commander who was pasturing his herds on Gargano Mountain. One day, his finest bull wandered off and he went in search of it. After many hours, he spotted it standing at the mouth of a cave in a remote part of the mountain. Enraged, he shot an arrow at the bull, but rather than hitting the animal, the arrow was rebounded by an unseen force and wounded the army commander in the foot. Shaken by this supernatural event, he sought advice from the local bishop, who spent three days in contemplative prayer. At the end of the third day, Michael appeared to the bishop saying, "I am the Archangel Michael and am always in the presence of God. The cave is sacred for me, I have chosen it; I myself am its watchful custodian . . . There where the rock opens wide the sins of man can be forgiven . . . What is asked for here in prayer will be granted. Therefore, go to the mountain and dedicate the grotto to the Christian religion."

On the appointed day, the townspeople marched in procession, sheltered from the glaring sun by a convocation of eagles soaring overhead. Arriving at the grotto, they discovered that an altar, covered by a vermilion cloth, had been erected. They took this as proof that the archangel had consecrated the cave before their arrival. Because it is the only place of worship

"Who is like God?"

— translation of the Hebrew phrase *Mi-cha-el*

✝

Saint Michael

not consecrated by human hand, this grotto is known as the Celestial Basilica. This became the first pilgrimage site in Christendom and is still much visited today.

The most famous shrine to Michael is Mont Saint-Michel in France. Situated on a rock rising a mile from the shore, this ancient monastery is an architectural wonder dating from the eleventh century. It houses a relic of the cloth that Michael is said to have left on the altar at Gargano, and it is in defense of this island that Michael's protection during war is much documented. One such battle took place in 1425, during the Hundred Years' War between England and France. In this decisive battle, 120 knights dedicated to Saint Michael held off eight thousand invading English troops. News of this heroic victory gave hope to a mostly demoralized French public. Joan of Arc's loyalty to Saint Michael has been attributed by many biographers to her youthful fascination with the incredible success of the aforementioned battle.

But Michael did not only extend his hand to war. In the early Church and in the East, Michael was considered a healing angel. He was beloved for the creation of sacred springs in Greece and Constantinople, and the Christians of Egypt placed the Nile River under his patronage. In the sixth century, as a plague devastated Rome, Pope Gregory I saw a vision of Michael sheathing a bloody sword over Emperor Hadrian's tomb. He interpreted this as a sign that Rome was under the archangel's protection and that the plague would soon end. In gratitude, he had a church built over the tomb, renaming it Castel San Angelo (Castle of the Holy Angel). It soon became customary for the chronically ill to spend the night in this church on certain feast days, invoking the archangel for a cure. By the Middle Ages, September 29, the feast day Michael shares with the archangels Gabriel and Raphael, became a holy day of obligation. This day, known as Michelmas Day, was set aside for settling quarterly rents and choosing magistrates in England, where the archangel's cult was once very strong. In early times there were more than four hundred recorded sightings of Michael throughout the British Isles, and he is still the patron of that nation.

As the representative of the forces of God, Michael was once considered a powerful patron to put one's country under. Today, he represents the forces of good versus evil that are a constant presence in the world. That first battle between Michael and Lucifer is ever continuing, although on a constantly changing stage. They are perpetually at war to win over as many souls as possible.

‡

Saint Michael

In art, Michael is most frequently portrayed vanquishing Lucifer. Since Michael is said to weigh the souls of the dead to decide who gets into heaven, he is always depicted with a set of scales. For this reason he is the patron of greengrocers. Many shops and stores display a statue of Michael as a reminder that the shopkeeper is under his protection. Because of his great military achievements against Lucifer and his constant vigilance and defense of the faithful, he is also the patron of policemen and firemen and those who protect the general public. Because his shrines are on the coasts of countries he is invoked by mariners for protection while on the seas. His cult was particularly strong in Germany, where his similarity to the god Wotan caused the conversion of pagans. In Gaul, he was accepted as a replacement for the god Mercury.

Prayer to Saint Michael the Archangel
Saint Michael the Archangel,
Defend us in battle.
Be our protection against the wickedness and snares of the devil.
May God rebuke him, we humbly pray;
And do thou, O Prince of the heavenly host,
By the power of God,
Thrust into hell
Satan and all evil spirits
Who wander through the world
For the ruin of souls.
Amen.

☩

Saint Michael

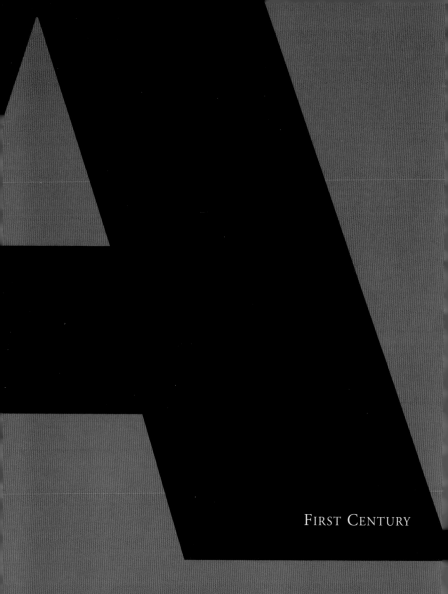

Saint Anne

Feast Day: July 26

Patron of: Brittany, Canada, broom makers, cabinetmakers, grandparents, housewives, lace makers, miners, pregnancy, rain, those without children

Invoked for: finding a husband, a good death, help in raising children, protection in pregnancy and childbirth, protection in sea storms, protection in thunderstorms

Symbols: book, golden gate, throne

Saint Anne is beloved for being the mother of the Virgin Mary, and through her marriages, grandmother to Jesus and many of His apostles. Her story was first told in the second century as part of The Protevangelium of James, a gospel written about the early life of Jesus Christ. Widely read by early Christians, it was never accepted as part of the New Testament canon. However, her place as matriarch of a spiritual lineage has been embraced. According to this ancient text, Anne and her husband, Joachim, had a childless marriage for almost twenty years. One day, Joachim presented his offering for the dedication of a new temple and was shunned by a priest, who declared that their childlessness was a curse from God. In humiliation, Joachim fled to the wilderness for forty days of prayer. When Anne heard the disturbing news, she begged the Lord to allow her to conceive and promised to dedicate any child she might have to the service of the Lord.

Suddenly, an angel appeared to Joachim in the hinterland and said, "Delayed conceptions and infertile childbearing are all the more wonderful! Your wife will bear you a daughter and you will call her Mary. As you have vowed, she will be consecrated to the Lord at infancy and filled with the Holy Spirit from her mother's womb." He was told to go back to the city and meet his wife at the golden gate of Jerusalem. A distraught Anne, with no knowledge of where her husband had gone, was visited by the same angel, who told her, "You will meet your husband at the city gate, and this will be a sign that your prayers are answered."

Anne and Joachim were overjoyed to see each other, and Mary was conceived. When their precious only child reached the age of three, they honored their pledge to dedicate her to God. Not without tears, they left Mary at the

‡

Saint Anne

temple to be raised in religious service. Years later, Mary became the mother of Jesus Christ.

Anne's life of service to God did not end with the one great gift of her daughter. According to an early account of her life, when Joachim died, Anne married his brother Cleophas, with whom she had another daughter. This child was also named Mary and became the mother of James the Lesser, Joseph the Just, Simon, and Jude. Anne later married again and had another daughter who gave birth to James the Greater and John the Evangelist.

Saint Anne did not live to see the torment and execution of Christ. However, even in death she continued to play an important part in the lives of early Christians. Sometime after the resurrection of Christ, Mary Magdalene, her brother Lazarus, and other apostles were driven from Jerusalem because of their faith. They journeyed by boat carrying the remains of Saint Anne and set ashore in Marseille, France. Her remains were taken farther inland from the coast to what is now Apt, France, where they were concealed in a crypt. These events were transcribed in the *Martyrology of Apt,* dating from the second century. Charlemagne consulted the text in an attempt to locate her body nearly seven hundred years later. All efforts appeared to be in vain until the reconsecration of the Cathedral of Apt. During this ceremony, a fourtenn-year-old deaf mute began striking the main altar with his staff, greatly disturbing those in attendance, including the emperor. Charlemagne was so impressed with the determination of the boy to draw attention to the altar that he gave orders to open its stairs after the mass. An underground door sealed with stones was uncovered. When these 11

"Joachim and Anne, how blessed a couple! All creation is indebted to you. For at your hands the Creator was offered a gift excelling all other gifts: a chaste mother who alone was worthy of Him."

— Saint John Damascene, seventh century

✠

Saint Anne

were removed, the boy led the group through the underground catacombs of the church to a wall, which he also struck with his staff. The company eagerly broke through the wall to find a crypt containing a casket of cypress wood. Inscribed on it were the words *Here lies the body of Blessed Anne, mother of the Virgin Mary*. Charlemagne had the recollection of these events written up, notarized, and sent to the pope in Rome. The original papers of this correspondence are still in existence today.

Because of these events, the Cathedral of Apt became an important pilgrimage site, and the cult of Saint Anne spread throughout France, becoming particularly strong in Brittany. Many Breton legends claim Saint Anne as a Breton queen who escaped a brutal husband. One legend supposes that angels led her to a ship that landed in Jerusalem, where she gave birth to the Virgin Mary.

She remained popular in other regions of the world as well. In the East, her feast was celebrated from the beginning of Christianity. As it spread through Western Europe, her patronage of fertility was extended to farmland and in Italy, agricultural workers referred to rain as "Saint Anne's gift;" in Germany, rain was referred to as "Saint Anne's dowery." Martin Luther wrote that he became a monk because of a promise he made to Saint Anne while he was caught in a terrifying thunderstorm. In the new world, Canada is still known as the "Land of Saint Anne." The story goes that in 1650 a group of sailors were caught in a storm on the Saint Lawrence River. As they were about to perish they invoked Saint Anne for help, promising to build a shrine to her wherever they first landed. They washed ashore on the north bank of the river at Beaupré, Quebec. Today, the Cathedral of Saint Anne de Beaupré now stands on that site and attracts millions of pilgrims from around the world. The chapel is filled with ex-votos donated to the church from people who have received miraculous healings.

Though not a biblical figure, Saint Anne was considered second only to Saint Joseph in importance by the early Eastern Church. Her role as a powerful matriach and grandmother to Jesus Christ served as a strong example in Western Europe, where communities depended on the wisdom and advice of the aged. To many, she is an accessible representative of a state of life, and she is invoked for a variety of favors that one might ask of a beloved grandmother. Because of her three marriages, young women ask her aid in finding a husband with the prayer "Saint Anne, find me a man."

The Hebrew name for Anne is Hannah, which means "grace." A common saying is "All Annes are beautiful" and because of this the name Anne became the most popular girl's name in Central Europe during the nineteenth century. Adding "Anne" after a girl's name is still common practice, particularly the combination of Mary Anne. Canada and Brittany, France, hold major celebrations in Saint Anne's honor on her feast day.

‡

Saint Anne

Anne's patronage of the sea and storms stems from the voyage her remains made with Lazarus and Mary Magdalene. She is frequently depicted with an open book, instructing her daughter, the Virgin Mary. Because her womb held Mary she is the patron of miners who dig up secret treasures. Since tabernacles were once made only of wood, and her womb was considered a human tabernacle, she is also the patron of carpenters and cabinetmakers.

Prayer to Saint Anne

O glorious Saint Anne, you are filled with compassion for those who invoke you and with love for those who suffer!
Heavily burdened with the weight of my troubles,
I cast myself at your feet and humbly beg of you to take the present intention which I recommend to you in your special care [state intention].

Please recommend it to your daughter, the Blessed Virgin Mary, and place it before the throne of Jesus, so that He may bring it to a happy issue.

Continue to intercede for me until my request is granted.
But, above all, obtain for me the grace one day to see my God face to face, and with you and Mary and all the saints to praise and bless Him for all eternity. Amen.

O Jesus, Holy Mary, Saint Anne, help me now and at the hour of my death.

Good Saint Anne, intercede for me.

✠

Saint Anne

Saint Joseph

Feast Day: March 19
Patron of: Austria, Belgium, Bohemia, Canada, China, Croatia, Korea, Mexico, Peru, Vietnam, carpenters, Catholic Church, families, fathers, homeless, pregnant women, workers
Invoked for: family protection, to find work, a happy death, to sell a home
Invoked against: doubt, hesitation
Symbols: Baby Jesus, carpenter's tools, flowering branch, lily

A working man descended from royal lineage, Joseph is said to have been chosen by God to protect His greatest treasures, Jesus and Mary. In the few descriptions of him in the Gospels, Joseph never speaks, yet he is an extremely powerful force. He displays the depth of his faith by listening and quietly doing what he is told.

16   In the face of possible public scandal, he married Mary when she was pregnant with a child that was not his. When an angel told him that the child she had conceived was of the Holy Spirit, he accepted it. Then, when all citizens were required to register on the tax rolls, Joseph dutifully took a very pregnant Mary with him to Bethlehem. As the city was severely overcrowded, they could not find a proper place to sleep and that night Mary was forced to give birth in a stable. After Jesus' birth, the holy family settled back into Nazareth until an angel warned Joseph in a dream of the impending slaughter of the innocents and instructed him to flee with Mary and Jesus to Egypt. Without hesitation Joseph relinquished his business and home to take his wife and young son on a perilous journey to an unknown land. Following the angel's order, they stayed in Egypt for seven years, with Joseph caring for both the financial and spiritual needs of the Holy Family.

The final mention of Joseph is in the story of the twelve-year-old Jesus straying from his family during a pilgrimage to Jerusalem. It is believed that Joseph died well before Jesus began his public life, and his patronage for a good death stems from the probability that he was surrounded by Jesus and Mary as he lay on his deathbed.

While the gospels concern Joseph only in regard to his relationship to Jesus, other histories of Joseph passed down from the fifth century state that Joseph was a widower who had been married forty-nine years and had six

✝

Saint Joseph

children before his first wife died. When the priests announced that all unmarried men from the tribe of Juda were to be candidates to wed Mary, Joseph went to Jerusalem with great reluctance. He was elderly and did not think he should be seriously considered. While the other men presented themselves by putting their walking sticks on the altar, Joseph held back and did not participate. To everyone's amazement, the tip of his staff burst into a bloom of flowers, a sign from God that he was to be named the fiancé of Mary. This tale is where the early visual depictions of Joseph as an elderly man with a flowering branch come from. It was also thought in all probability he would have been older, as Joseph had to respect Mary's virginity throughout their marriage.

Despite the importance of Joseph in the life of Christ, his cult was only found in the East. It did not arrive in the West until the ninth century when he was honored in church as the Foster Father of Our Lord. The Carmelite order brought his cult to Europe when they were driven out of Jerusalem during the Crusades and the first church dedicated to him was in 1129 in Bologna, Italy. European evangelists recognized Joseph's reputation as the perfect father figure as useful in gaining conversions. Common people forced to put the needs of their family before personal ambition saw Joseph's life mirror their own.

His role of provider and father were the reasons many invoked him for help in caring for their own families. During the Middle Ages when drought and famine struck Sicily, residents throughout that island prayed to Saint Joseph for help. At midnight on March 19, Joseph's feast day, rain began pouring down, immediately followed by good weather. Sicilians have venerated Saint Joseph ever since by setting up altars and cooking special food and

> **"I know by experience that the glorious Saint Joseph assists us generally in all necessities. I never asked him for anything which he did not obtain for me."**
>
> — Saint Teresa of Ávila

✝

Saint Joseph

sweets, which are given to friends and to the poor. These festivities were adapted by the rest of Italy where Saint Joseph is greatly revered as well. There, it is believed that Saint Joseph is an extremely powerful intercessor, having the power to overturn natural law, because Jesus had to obey his earthly father while he was a boy, and would still do whatever Saint Joseph asked of him.

Perhaps the most ardent and famous devotee of Saint Joseph was Saint Teresa of Ávila. While reforming the Carmelite order in Spain, she chose him to be the patron of her Discalced Carmelite order. Because of his tradition of taking care of the needs of the Holy Family, she requested he do the same for her nuns. The custom of burying a Saint Joseph's statue on the grounds of a home to initiate its sale originates with Teresa of Ávila. When she was in need of more land to set up her religious houses, she had her nuns bury their Saint Joseph's medals in the ground. Over time others adapted this ritual, and these medals evolved into a statue of Saint Joseph that would be buried upside down until the house was sold, then dug up and taken to the new home. Today, even some non-Catholics do this as a superstitious rite, buying Saint Joseph's Home Sale Kits off the Internet.

But it is for the excellent example he gives as a provider for the family and working man that Saint Joseph is most honored. With the advent of the Industrial Revolution, and the new class of laborers it produced, patronage to Saint Joseph the Worker became universal. By the end of the nineteenth century, he was named patron of the Catholic Church out of gratitude for the care he took of Jesus.

Saint Joseph and baby Jesus

‡

Saint Joseph

In art, Saint Joseph is usually depicted with the infant Jesus. He sometimes has carpenter tools, and because of his chastity he carries a lily for purity. The flowering staff became a popular attribute for him because it is also the emblem of shepherd kings who forcefully defended their flock. This staff is also the ancestor of the bishop's crook. Because Joseph had to move on a moment's notice with the flight into Egypt and was responsible for providing shelter for his family, he is invoked for buying or selling a home. An additional feast day was declared for Saint Joseph as May 1, May Day to the rest of the world. In its attempt to combat communism, the Church dedicated this day set aside for the working man to the Patron of Workers.

Prayer for Saint Joseph's Intercession
Remember, O most chaste spouse of the Virgin Mary,
That never was it known that anyone who implored your help
and sought your intercession was left unassisted.
Full of confidence in your power,
I fly unto you and beg your protection.
Despise not, O foster father of the Redeemer,
My humble supplication, [request here]
but in your bounty, hear and answer me.
Amen.

✝

Saint Joseph

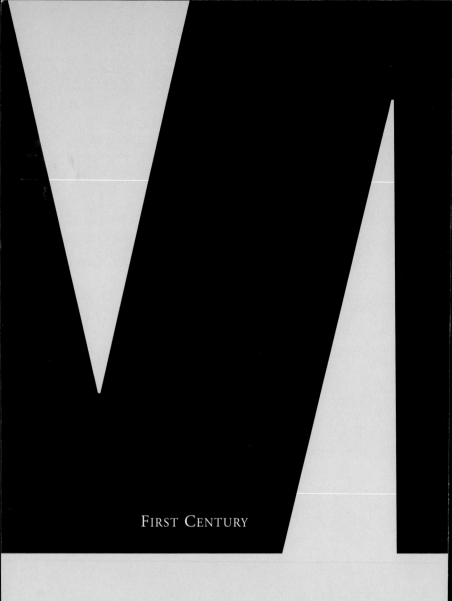

FIRST CENTURY

Saint Mary Magdalene
Apostle to the Apostles

Feast Day: July 22
Patron of: Provence, contemplatives, converts, gardeners, glove makers, hairdressers, penitents, perfumers, pharmacists, prisoners, reformed prostitutes
Invoked against: sexual temptation
Symbols: alabaster jar, long hair, skull

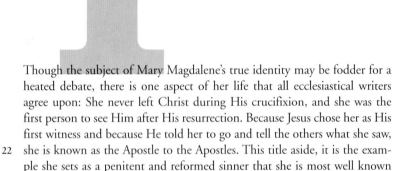

Though the subject of Mary Magdalene's true identity may be fodder for a heated debate, there is one aspect of her life that all ecclesiastical writers agree upon: She never left Christ during His crucifixion, and she was the first person to see Him after His resurrection. Because Jesus chose her as His first witness and because He told her to go and tell the others what she saw, she is known as the Apostle to the Apostles. This title aside, it is the example she sets as a penitent and reformed sinner that she is most well known and honored.

According to ancient Jewish texts, the seaside town of Magdala was known as a place of loose morals. This town was Mary's home, and she took its name as her own, signifying her unmarried state. It was said that Mary had wealth and took great pride in her appearance, enjoying luxuries and lapsing into promiscuity. Many shunned her because of her reputation for lewdness, and it is as this sinner that we are first introduced to her.

After Jesus had raised the son of a widow from the dead, a man named Simon invited him to be guest of honor at a dinner. While they were seated, a certain notorious woman walked into the room carrying an alabaster box. Weeping, she threw herself down and wiped Jesus' feet with her hair and then anointed them with the oil. Simon was outraged that Jesus would accept such tribute from someone so disgraceful. But instead of judging the woman, Jesus rebuked Simon, "Does thou see this woman? I entered into thy house–thou gave me no water for my feet. But she with tears has washed my feet, and with her hair has wiped them. Thou gave me no kiss. But she, since she came in, has not ceased to kiss my feet. My head with oil thou did not anoint but she with ointment has anointed my feet. Wherefore I say to thee: Many sins are forgiven her, because she has loved much. But to whom less is forgiven,

✝

Saint Mary Magdalene

he loves less." He then told the penitent woman to go in peace, all her sins were forgiven.

In the next chapter of Luke (8:2) he mentions the travels of Christ and his followers in Galilee, among them is "Mary called Magdalene, out of whom went seven devils." Luke also tells us that the day before Christ's entry into Jerusalem he dined with Lazarus and his sisters Martha and Mary. When Judas objects to the use of such expensive oil, he is rebuked by Christ, like Simon, for being so self-righteous. "...For the poor you have always with you ...but me you have not always..." Because in this story, Mary too wipes Jesus' feet with her hair and anoints them with oil in the same manner as the penitent woman, Catholics believe both women to be Mary Magdalene, whom after being exorcized by Christ became one of his greatest and most loyal followers.

Indeed, her loyalty to Jesus was unsurpassed even at His death. Unlike His other disciples, Mary never renounced Jesus or ran from Him. She stood with His mother until He was dead, helped take Him down from the cross and wept outside of His tomb. On Easter morning it was Mary Magdalene who returned at dawn to keep a vigil. When she found the great stone covering the tomb rolled away, she ran back to tell Peter and the others that someone had taken Jesus' body. They ran ahead of her, saw the open tomb, and left.

But it was Mary Magdalene who stayed behind, searching the tomb and weeping. Two angels dressed in white appeared to her and asked why she was weeping. "They have taken my Lord, and I know not where they have laid him," she responded. A gardener asked her the same question and she begged the man to tell her where Christ's body might be found. "Mary," said the man, and she suddenly knew this man was not a gardener. She was talking to

"Touch me not; for I am not yet ascended to My Father; but go to my brethren, and say unto them, I ascend unto My Father, and your Father; and *to* My God, and your God."

— Christ to Mary Magdalene according to John 20:17

✝

Saint Mary Magdalene

the risen Christ. When she went to embrace him, he told her, "Touch me not!" (The phrase *Noli me tangere* in the Latin bible). Mary spread the good news to the disciples—the last action the gospels recorded of Mary Magdalene.

The rest of her life story was written in the early Middle Ages. It is said that after the resurrection of Christ, political leaders in Israel tried to quash the cult that was rapidly growing around Him. These leaders placed Mary Magdalene; her sister, Martha; their brother, Lazarus; and other followers in a rudderless boat, in hopes that they would perish at sea. Divine Providence brought them to the coast of Marseilles, France. There they had much success converting the local people to Christianity. Mary took her apostolic mission to Provence and was greeted with equal enthusiasm. After converting the king and helping to install a bishop, she retired to a cave to live out the last thirty years of her life as a penitent. Her hair grew long enough to cover her naked body, and she repented for her previous deeds as a sinner. Once a day, angels would carry her to heaven, where she received her "daily sustenance," which took the place of earthly food. Eventually her death drew near, and she sent for Maximinus, the bishop she had installed years earlier. She received the eucharist and died in tears.

Early French ecclesiastical writers claimed Mary Magdalene and her family as their evangelists. Since they were favorites of Christ, this divine favoritism then extended to France and the French people. Miraculous discoveries of her relics abounded from Provence to Burgundy. The cathedral at Vézelay was dedicated to her in the twelfth century and became the center of her cult and an important stop on the pilgrimage to Campostela. Her feast, falling in the heart of summer, was happily celebrated throughout France.

To the people of the Middle Ages, Mary Magdalene was a wildly glamorous figure, a beautiful woman with long, red hair. She presented an alternative to the image of an ever pious saint. Here was a woman who had enjoyed luxuries, made mistakes, and tried to redeem herself. As towns grew into cities, they began to face an onslaught of urban problems such as prostitution. Though there is no mention in the Bible of Mary Magdalene ever being a prostitute, preachers invented lurid tales of her youthful sexual indiscretions. That God could extend forgiveness to such a willful, wayward creature gave hope to everyone for their own forgiveness. Homes for reformed prostitutes took her as their patron, and the word *magdalene* became a description for a fallen woman. It was not until the twentieth century that Mary Magdalene's role as a penitent and devoted follower of Christ was stressed.

‡

Saint Mary Magdalene

Always a popular subject for artists, Mary Magdalene is always depicted as a beautiful, sorrowful woman with long hair. In some images she carries the alabaster unguent jar and in others a skull is present, the symbol of the penitent to remind us of how we are all going to end up. The English word *maudlin* is a derivative of *magdalene*. Oxford University has a famous college named for her. Because she loved luxury before her conversion and bought expensive unguents after it, she is the patron of such trades as glove makers, hair-dressers, and perfumers. Since devils were cast out of her, she is the patron of prisoners who cast off their chains. Because Christ appeared to her as a gardener she is the patron of the profession. Her knowledge and use of unguents also makes her the patron of pharmacists.

Prayer to Saint Mary Magdalene
Saint Mary Magdalene, woman of many sins,
Who by conversion became the beloved of Jesus,
Thank you for your witness that Jesus forgives
through the miracle of love.

You, who already possess eternal happiness
in His glorious presence,
please intercede for me, so that someday
I may share in the same everlasting joy.
Amen.

✝

Saint Mary Magdalene

Saint Jude

Apostle

Feast Day: October 28
Patron of: impossible causes
Invoked for: help in times of desperation
Symbols: Club, cloth with image of Jesus, flame over head,

Saint Jude was one of the original twelve apostles of Jesus. During his lifetime, his compassion and love for others was profoundly evident. Now, thousands of years after his death, his relief aid in seemingly hopeless situations ensures his place as one of the most popular and invoked saints in the world.

Jude Thaddeus was said to be a cousin of Jesus and the brother of James the Lesser. As an apostle of Christ, Jude learned firsthand the power of God to bring about healing and protection for what some might call "lost causes." The most intriguing example can be found in the legends of Edessa (a city in Mesopotamia). As the story goes, King Abgar suffered greatly from leprosy and, desperate for relief, wrote a letter to Christ, which read, "I have heard about you and the cures you effect, that you do this without medicaments or herbs, and that with a word you cause the blind to see, the lame to walk, lepers to be cleansed, and the dead to live again. Having heard all this, I have decided in my mind that you are either a god and have come down from heaven to do what you do, or you are the Son of God and so do these things . . ."

Jesus was happy that King Abgar believed in Him without even seeing Him; however, He did not have time to visit the king. When the king realized he would never see Christ Himself, he sent an artist to draw a portrait. The artist was so overcome with the radiance emanating from Christ's eyes, his hands shook and he could not accomplish his task. Jesus took a cloth and wiped His face with it, leaving His image imprinted in the cloth. Jude was sent back to Edessa to present this portrait to the king, who rubbed it on his own body and was instantly cured of his disease.

In a different version of the story, Jude presented the burial cloth of Christ to King Agbar by carrying the precious material seared with Christ's image folded up as a portrait. The king was cured when he touched the shroud. His

‡

Saint Jude

subsequent baptism by Jude established Christianity in Edessa. Jude's role as a helper to the despondent was sealed, as was his influence in the Mideast region of the world. The shroud, of course, has become known as the Holy Shroud of Turin.

After the death, resurrection, and ascension of Christ, Jude and the apostle Simon were sent back to Mesopotamia (present-day Iraq), Persia, Armenia, and southern Russia to preach. The men became popular with the local population for their keen intellect, clever dialogue, and the amusing ways in which they outwitted sorcerers and magicians in public discourses and arguments. When invited to choose, as was the custom of the day, how their losing antagonists were to be executed, Jude and Simon would reply, "We are not here to kill the living but to bring the dead back to life." They would then joyfully preach the message of Christ, converting thousands at a time.

Jude and Simon were not without detractors, however, and in the Epistle of Jude, his only writings to survive him, Jude exhorts recent converts in the East in A.D. 60, to stay strong in the face of persecution and to persevere through harsh and difficult circumstances. These persecutions caught up with both Simon and Jude just five years later when they were martyred together for their evangelizing. Today, their relics are buried under the main altar of Saint Peter's Basilica.

Over the centuries, Saint Jude became confused with Judas Iscariot, the apostle who betrayed Christ for thirty pieces of silver. In many instances, to avoid this confusion, he is referred to as "Thaddeus" in the writings of the evangelists. Because he shared a name with such a notorious character, few 29 Christians invoked Saint Jude for help. The mystical saints Bernard of Clairvaux in the twelfth century and Bridget of Sweden in the fifteenth century were exceptions. According to a vision, Jesus told Saint Bridget of Sweden to dedicate an altar to Saint Jude, because "in accordance with his surname, Thaddeus [meaning generous or loving] he will show himself most willing to give help."

"...in accordance with his surname Thaddeus [meaning generous or loving], he will show himself most willing to give help."

—Saint Bridget of Sweden, fifteenth century

‡

Saint Jude

Few Catholics took these words seriously until the nineteenth century when a tradition began that when Saint Jude would answer the most impossible of prayers, the petitioner in turn, must thank the saint in a public way. The advent of inexpensive newspapers made this obligation possible and to this day, weekly and daily periodicals all have their share of "Thank you Saint Jude" personal ads. Perhaps the grandest gesture of public thanks to this saint is the world-famous Saint Jude's Children Hospital in Memphis, Tennessee. It was built by the entertainer Danny Thomas as a tribute to Jude for answering his prayers when he was struggling to support his family. This hospital serves children with hopelessly incurable diseases and has become a groundbreaking research institution, saving innumerable young lives on its premises and even more internationally through its discoveries. From its great success, the name Saint Jude has become a common name for research hospitals all over the world.

Shrine of Saint Jude in New Orleans

☩

Saint Jude

Since he was present at the Pentecost, Saint Jude is usually depicted with the flame of the Holy Spirit over his head. His principal attribute is the cloth with Christ's image, sometimes displayed on his body in a medallion form. He carries the club or axe he was beaten to death with and also displays the palms of the martyr.

Prayer to Saint Jude
Saint Jude, glorious Apostle, faithful servant and
    friend of Jesus,
The name of the traitor has caused you to be forgotten
    by many,
But the true Church invokes you universally as the patron
Of things despaired of; pray for me,
    that I may receive the consolations and the help of
    heaven in all my necessities, tribulations, and sufferings,
    particularly (here make your request) and that I
    may bless God with the elect throughout eternity.
St. Jude, Apostle, martyr, and cousin of our Lord Jesus Christ,
    intercede for us.
Amen.

31

✠

Saint Jude

SECOND OR THIRD CENTURY

Saint Cecilia

Feast Day: November 22
Patron of: music, musicians, musical instrument makers, poets, Rome Academy of Music, singers
Symbols: lute, martyrs palms, organ, roses

**S**he has inspired masterpieces in every artistic discipline, and the popularity of her cult spans from ancient to modern times. Yet little is known about Cecilia besides the fact that she was a rich young Roman girl martyred in her home in Trastevere.

Cecilia came from the senatorial family Coecilia, a family prominent in Rome's ancient history. Although Christianity was illegal, her mother raised her as a Christian, and Cecilia secretly took a vow of chastity. Her father, not taking his daughter's faith seriously, arranged a marriage for her to a nobleman named Valerian. As musicians played for the guests, Cecilia begged God to help her keep her vow.

On their wedding night, Cecilia told Valerian she had a guardian angel with her that only she could see and warned him that the angel would be upset if she were touched in an impure way. When he asked to see the angel, she directed him to go out and be baptized. Valerian did as she asked and on his return, he found Cecilia praying in her room next to an angel with flaming wings. In his hands, the angel held two wreaths made of roses and lilies. After crowning the couple, the angel vanished.

When Valerian's brother Tibertius entered the home, he was astounded at the rare beauty and fragrance of the flowers. Upon hearing of Cecilia and her guardian angel, he too was baptized. Valerian and Tibertius became active in the Christian community, making lavish gifts to the poor and burying martyrs slain for their faith. These actions came to the attention of the Roman Prefect, who demanded they make sacrifices to the Roman gods to prove their patriotism. When the two men refused, they were executed. Cecilia then had them buried together in the same tomb owned by her family.

Cecilia was also put on trial and condemned to death for refusing to

☩

Saint Cecilia

renounce her faith. However, because she came from an illustrious family, Cecilia could not be executed in public. Instead, she was shut up in her sudarium, the steam room of her bath house. The vents were sealed, and the furnaces were heated seven times higher than their normal limit in order to suffocate her. Cecilia was discovered the next day, happily praying, seemingly untouched by the hellish atmosphere of the room. The Prefect remained undeterred by her miraculous survival, and an executioner was dispatched to decapitate her. Hitting her three times with an axe, he was unable to kill her. Because Roman law decreed that three blows with the axe was the legal limit an executioner could use to kill a prisoner, Cecilia was left to bleed to death on the floor of her home. Crowds flocked to visit her as she prayed. She disbursed her worldly goods to the poor, and she left her house to the pope to be used as a church. When she finally died three days later, she was buried in the catacombs of Saint Callixtus.

This story was recorded hundreds of years after her death, in the fifth century's *Acts of Cecilia*, which detailed her suffering and served as an inspiration for early Christians. At that time, her home was one of the first churches in Rome. Cecilia was so well regarded that her feast day was widely celebrated and there were five different masses held in her honor.

In 821, Pope Paschal decided to repair the crumbling ruin of her church. Wanting to have a relic of the saint's, he searched the catacombs. He could not find her remains, but in a dream Cecilia encouraged his search, saying that, in actuality, he had been very near her body. In the neighboring catacomb of Pratextarus, it was discovered that many bodies of the original martyrs had been moved to prevent thievery. One, a perfectly preserved young woman, wrapped in gold, with bloody rags at her feet, was thought to be Cecilia.

Blessed Cecilia, appear in visions To all musicians, appear and inspire: Translated Daughter, come down and startle Composing mortals with immortal fire.

— from "Anthem for St. Cecilia's Day" by W. H. Auden

‡

Saint Cecilia

Among other martyrs with her were Valerian and Tiburtius. These relics along with those of the ancient popes Urbanus and Lucius were installed in the altar of the Church of Saint Cecilia in Trastevere.

During the early Renaissance when many ancient texts were being translated, the lines in her *Acts* that read *"Cantantibus organis illa in corde suo soi domino decantabat"* ("While musicians played at her nuptials, she sang only in her heart to God") were misconstrued to say that Cecilia herself played the organ at her own wedding. From this grew the legend that she not only could play every single musical instrument, but that Cecilia even invented the organ. When an early sixteenth-century Florentine musical academy named Cecilia as their patron saint, other musical organizations followed suit, including the Academy of Music in Rome. This is the beginning of Cecilia's patronage of music and poetry. From the Renaissance forward, all visual depictions of Cecilia featured musical instruments. In England it became a tradition to celebrate Saint Cecilia's Day with musical concerts, and many great composers have written compositions in her honor.

It was in the spirit of this newfound respect for the arts brought on by the Renaissance that a renovation of Saint Cecilia's in Trastevere was undertaken in 1599. When the relics of Cecilia and the other martyrs were found beneath the altar, it became a major event in the cultural world. One of the official witnesses to the uncovering of the relics was sculptor Stefano Maderno. According to those who were there, Cecilia was still incorrupt and his work, which resides in the church, is an uncanny physical likeness of the saint. Though that was almost 1,500 years after her death, the streets of Rome were thronged with thousands who came to honor her. On November 22, 1599, accompanied by forty-two cardinals, the pope came to her basilica to celebrate a Solemn High Mass. Cecilia's remains were then reinterred beneath the high altar.

Though the story of Cecilia has always been considered a pious legend, future restorations of her church in Trastevere unearthed the bathroom of a private Roman home from ancient times. The ruins were complete with a boiler and lead pipes buried two levels underneath the building, presenting the feasibility that there might be more truth in the story of her life than was first considered possible. What cannot be denied is that Cecilia had captured the public imagination, becoming a popular subject for painters such as Raphael, Delaroche, and Poussin. Handel, Gounod, Scarlatti, and Benjamin Britten are just a few of the composers who have written musical celebrations of her. Poets from Chaucer to Auden have written odes to her. And today, it is customary for musicians to invoke her aid for a good performance.

‡

Saint Cecilia

In art, Cecilia is represented holding or playing a musical instrument. Sometimes she is surrounded by angels. Martyrs' palms, lilies for purity, and roses for the wreath she and her husband were given by the angel on their wedding night often appear with Cecilia.

Musician's Prayer to Saint Cecilia
Heroic martyr who stayed faithful to Jesus your divine bridegroom,
Give us faith to rise above our persecutors and to see in them the
Image of our Lord.
We know that you were a musician and we are told that you
Heard angels sing.
Inspire musicians to gladden the hearts of people by filling the air
With God's gift of music and reminding them of the Divine
Musician
Who created all beauty.
Amen.

☩

Saint Cecilia

A.D. 269

Saint Valentine

Feast Day: February 14
Patron of: beekeepers, engaged couples, greeting card
manufacturers, happy marriages, love, lovers, young people
Invoked against: epilepsy, fainting, plague
Symbols: birds, martyrs' palms, rose, sun, sword

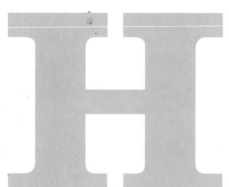His feast day is embedded in Western civilization. His name has become synonymous with a certain type of romantic card, yet few realize that Valentine actually existed. As a saint, his first great work was to unite young couples in marriage.

In the year A.D. 269, when the Roman Empire was under constant attack from barbarian tribes, Emperor Marcus Aurelius Claudius issued an edict outlawing marriage for young men. He speculated that more soldiers would join the legions to defend it if they were unfettered by wives and children. Valentine was a respected healer and priest in the outlawed Christian faith. He had great sympathy for those young couples whose plans for a life together were shattered by the state and he encouraged anyone who wished to wed to come to him to be married in secret. He was arrested and imprisoned in Rome for defying the emperor. But his reputation as a learned man remained untarnished and many of his followers would visit him in prison for counseling; others came for health cures. Personally afflicted with epilepsy, Valentine was particularly drawn to treating those also suffering from the disease.

The jailer, having witnessed many successful healings at Valentine's cell door, asked the saint to treat his daughter, who had been blind since birth. During her subsequent visits to the prison, Valentine read to the girl, taught her mathematics, and beautifully described the natural world. Valentine's wisdom and kindness so impressed the jailer and his family that they converted to Christianity despite the fact that the young girl remained blind. This conversion established Valentine's status as a true threat to the state, a charge punishable by death. His execution came on February 14, the eve of the Roman festival of Lupercalia. Valentine was beaten with clubs and then beheaded. Before his sentence was carried out, however, he sent a yellow crocus

‡

Saint Valentine

to the jailer's daughter enclosed with a note that read, "With love, from your Valentine." The bright color of this flower was the first thing she ever saw, her eyesight having been miraculously restored. She is said to have planted an almond tree on Valentine's grave, and to this day the almond tree is considered a symbol of friendship and devotion.

Valentine was buried on the Flaminian Way in a catacomb that still bears his name. A church was dedicated to him there in A.D. 496. The wall of the city, the original Flaminian Gate, was a pilgrim's first stop upon entering Rome and was known as Porta S. Valentino until the seventeenth century, when it was renamed Porta del Popolo. In the ninth century, relics of the early martyrs were removed from the catacombs and transferred to local Roman churches. Valentine, too, was reinterred in the church. His body was moved to the church of Saint Praxedes, very near his original burial place. Many cities besides Rome claim his relics, among them Terni, Italy; Madrid, Spain; Dublin, Ireland; Glasgow, Scotland; and Rocamador, France.

It is no coincidence that the liturgical feast day of the patron saint of love falls on the eve of Lupercalia, an erotic Roman fertility festival. It was common practice for church holidays to coopt pagan celebrations. The Romans considered this the official beginning of spring, a time of reawakening fertility and warming weather. One of the activities held in honor of the goddess Februata Juno consisted of the city's bachelors drawing the names of unmarried women out of an urn. They would then become a couple for the rest of the year, with many of these matches resulting in marriage. In twelfth-century southern France, this practice was reawakened as part of the Langue d'Oc poetry movement. This was a time when art and literature took on a heightened importance to the ruling classes. Noble youths known as gallants wrote missives of love they called *galantines*. The local pronunciation confused this with the word *valentine* and Valentines clubs sprang up. On February 14, after a Mass in honor of Love, a silver casket containing the names of unmarried local men was presented to the single women in town. The men whose names each woman drew was required to

For this we sent on Seynt Valentyne's day When every fowle cometh ther to choose his mate.

— from the fourteenth-century poem "Parliament of Fowles" by Geoffrey Chaucer

‡

Saint Valentine

be the guardian of that lady, providing her with flowers, poems, and gifts throughout the year. He was to guard her honor chivalrously. Marriage between these Valentines was strictly forbidden.

Because of the wide dispersal of his remains, the cult of Saint Valentine became extremely popular in Northern Italy, southern France, and England. His head, which was reputed to be in England, was said to bestow incredible miracles and healings on those who kissed it. Since the middle of February was considered the time of year when birds began to pair, the English, like the Romans a thousand years before them, looked upon this as the beginning of mating season. Celebrating the Feast of Saint Valentine by citing the fidelity of doves seems to be an English tradition. The oldest valentine note in existence today was written by Charles, Duke of Orleans, to his wife in 1415, while he was imprisoned in the Tower of London.

By the middle of the nineteenth century, sending and receiving anonymous Valentine's cards and poems declaring one's love became common in both America and England. By then, the story of the saint who had inspired this industry might have faded away, but his name and feast day is celebrated universally.

Old greeting card

✝

Saint Valentine

In art Saint Valentine is sometimes depicted as a bishop since it is believed he could possibly be the same person as the first martyred bishop of Interamna (Terni, Italy). Frequently a pair of doves symbolizing faithful unions, the sword he was martyred with, the sun of honest knowledge, and the rose of ardent love can be found as part of his portrait as well as martyrs' palms. Because he suffered from epilepsy, he is invoked against that disease, as well as fainting spells.

Prayer to Saint Valentine
O glorious advocate and protector,
Saint Valentine,
look with pity upon our wants,
hear our requests,
attend to our prayers,
relieve by your intercession the miseries
under which we labor,
and obtain for us the divine blessing,
that we may be found worthy to join you
in praising the Almighty for all
eternity; through the merits of
Our Lord Jesus Christ.
Amen.

43

✝

Saint Valentine

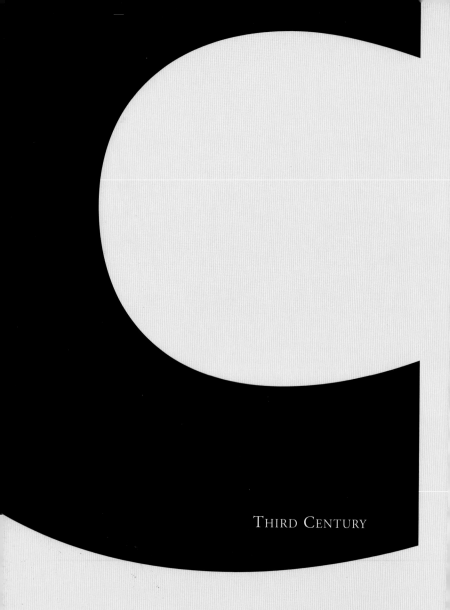

Saint Christopher
One of the Fourteen Holy Helpers

Feast Day: July 25
Patron of: athletes, couriers, gardeners, ferrymen, fruit growers,
fruit venders, motorists, pilgrims, porters, postal workers, railway
workers, taxi drivers, travelers
Invoked against: death, floods, hail, sudden hurricanes, plague
Symbols: carrying the Child Jesus, flowering staff

A standard image in automobiles and taxicabs, Saint Christopher is an unavoidable presence in modern society. He is the first saint that many non-Catholics come in contact with, and his cult has faded and been resurrected over a span of two thousand years. The stories of Saint Christopher are unique and fantastic. In the West, the story begins with a fearsome giant named Reprobus.

46

Born to a tribe in North Africa, Reprobus was so proud of his great physical prowess that he vowed to serve only the greatest king in the world. He put himself in service to a ruler whom he believed to be supreme, but he soon noticed that this king trembled and crossed himself at the mention of the devil. Witnessing the king's fear, he realized that a more powerful leader yet reigned. He left the king's court, found the devil, and put himself in his service. One day, while traveling with the devil and his army, they saw a cross on the road. The devil abruptly left this path and led them through the desert. When Reprobus saw that the devil was frightened, he demanded to know the reason. "There was a man named Christ who was nailed to a cross," he was told. "And when I see the sign of his cross, I am filled with terror and I run away!"

Reprobus left in disgust and set out to find this Jesus Christ, who could make the devil quake in fear. In his travels he came across a hermit who lived besides a dangerous river. This hermit was a known Christian who spent his days guiding travelers over the rushing water. When Reprobus asked the hermit how he could join Christ's service, the hermit suggested that the mighty giant take on the task of carrying travelers across the dangerous river currents. Reprobus gladly accepted this simple solution. He set up camp near the river and found a long pole to act as his steadying staff in the raging water.

‡

Saint Christopher

For a few days he carried travelers on his back through the currents. It came to pass that one day he heard the voice of a small child requesting to be carried across the river. He left his shelter but found no one there. He heard the voice a second time and still saw no one. The third time the child called, Reprobus again stepped outside and to his surprise saw a child standing on the riverbank. When the boy again requested to be carried over, the giant easily picked up the child, put him on his shoulders, and began walking across the river. To his astonishment, as he neared the heavy current, the child's weight seemed to increase. As the water grew rougher, the child grew heavy as lead. Engulfed in rapids and struggling to remain upright, Reprobus was sure they would both drown. When he finally reached the other shore, Reprobus put the boy down and admonished him, "My boy, you put me in great danger, and you weighed so much that if I had the whole world on my back I could not have felt it a heavier burden!" To his amazement, the child replied, "You were not only carrying the whole world, you had Him who created the world upon your shoulders! I am Christ your king, to whom you render service by doing the work you do here." The child then baptized him with the water from the river and told him that when Reprobus returned home, he was to plant his staff in the earth. "The next day you will find it bearing fruit as a form of proof of my identity." The child then vanished. Reprobus returned home and did what he was told. As promised, the next day he found his staff bearing the leaves and fruit of a palm tree. From that day on he took the name Christopher, which means "Christ bearer."

The story continues, and the powerful message that Christopher's flowering staff represented converted many to Christianity. The king, threatened by Christopher's masterly ability to relate to the common people, had the humble servant brought before him. The king said that Christopher was a fool to take the name of a crucified man as his leader. If he would denounce Christ, Christopher would be granted entrance into the king's service, and his life would be spared. When Christopher refused, the king ordered him tortured and shot with arrows. As four hundred archers aimed at the giant, one stray arrow turned in midair and went through the king's eye. Christopher told

"You were not only carrying the whole world, you had Him who created the world upon your shoulders!"

—Christ Child to Christopher

‡

Saint Christopher

him not to worry. He said that upon his death, the king should rub some of Christopher's shed blood into his eye and vision would be restored. Upon these words, Christopher was beheaded and the tyrant took some of the blood, rubbing it into the injured eye, saying, "In the name of God and Saint Christopher." When his vision was restored, the king immediately converted to Christinaity, along with those who had witnessed these events.

In the West, the story of Saint Christopher is taken as a fable for Christians to teach them to figuratively "bear Christ" in every aspect of their lives. In the East, however, the story differs. There, Christopher was known as a member of a warrior tribe of dog-headed cannibals, and traditional Orthodox iconography depicts him as a man with a dog's head. This is thought to be a literal interpretation of the Greco-Roman tradition of describing all foreigners from outside of the empire as cannibals or dog-headed. In truth, the historic Christopher was most likely from Berber tribes that resided in Libya. Many speculate he is the same person as the saint known as Menas, who always carried a picture of Christ near his heart. This holy man was martyred in Antioch and then taken to Alexandria to be honored by the Coptic Christians.

Despite the different tales of his origin, Saint Christopher is best known for his Western roots. His act of healing toward the king, his murderer, and his protection of travelers led to his adoption both as an intercessor for the sick and for those responsible for the safety of others.

Saint Christoper is often grouped with other saints thought to offer intercession of healing. Collectively known as the Fourteen Holy Helpers, each of these saints specializes in curing different parts of the body. Christopher was added to this group during the Middle Ages when the Black Plague raged through Europe. At this time, paintings of Saint Christopher appeared on the outside of many churches and village public walls because it was thought that anyone who saw his image would be safe from death that day. After the plague had run its course, these images became welcome sights to religious pilgrims, who found assurance in his protection of them along the road.

In the twentieth century, the cult of Saint Christopher saw great resurgence. As the patron saint of travelers and those who transport people, medallions bearing his image became prevalent, especially with the advent of the automobile. In the United States this tradition was introduced by European immigrants and became so popular that even many non-Catholics have a Saint Christopher medallion in their vehicle for protection.

Medal

‡

Saint Christopher

Because of his flowering staff, Saint Christopher is also the patron saint of gardeners and those who buy and sell fruit. Since he carried and delivered many to safety, he is the patron of ferrymen and postal workers. Because he worked in such violent currents, he is invoked against the violence of water such as floods and hail. Being endowed with great strength and physical perfection, he is also the patron of athletes. In art, Saint Christopher is always depicted carrying the Christ Child, his staff at his side.

Traveler's Prayer to Saint Christopher
O Saint Christopher, hear our prayer,
Keep me in your loving care.
Whatever the perils of the way,
Let me not add to them this day.
So to our caution and attention,
We add a prayer for your protection,
And beg God's blessing on this journey,
That we may travel safely near and far.
Amen.

49

✝

Saint Christopher

A.D. 283–304

Saint Lucy

Feast Day: December 13
Patron of: Syracuse, the blind, cutlers, electricians, glaziers, gondoliers, oculists, peasants, writers
Invoked for: clarity
Invoked against: dysentery, epidemics, eye disease, hemorrhages, throat ailments
Symbols: holding her eyes on a dish, martyrs' palms, sword, oxen

Saint Lucy was a privileged young woman who chose a state of enlightenment over the prosperous, respectable life she was expected to lead in Roman society. One of the early virgin martyrs, her quiet but steadfast rebellion against civil authorities earned her an excruciating death that became a triumphant example of everlasting life, hastening the overthrow of the emperor and the legalization of Christianity.

Born in Siracusa, Sicily, Lucy was a young Christian woman of Greek ancestry. She held a deep spiritual belief that one must remain pure to be a true conduit of the Holy Spirit. Lucy secretly vowed to remain a virgin, even while her widowed mother arranged her marriage to a wealthy pagan nobleman. Secrecy was necessary at this time in history. Christianity was looked upon as a threat by the Roman emperor. Because so many soldiers in the empire had converted, officials feared these Christians would follow the tenets of Christ over their military leaders. The state insisted that it was a man's duty to serve his nation militarily and a woman's duty to marry and bear children. When a girl refused to do this, she was considered a traitor to the empire. Thus, consecrating one's virginity to Christ was more of a bold and revolutionary stance against the state than a private act of devotion.

Lucy, therefore, did not immediately tell her mother of her decision. Instead, the two women traveled to the tomb of the virgin martyr Saint Agatha in Catania some fifty miles away. Agatha had become the patron of Catania after her veil stopped the deadly flow of Mount Etna's lava from entering the town. She was credited with so many miracles since her martyrdom thirty-five years prior, that Christians, Jews, and pagans alike were drawn to her tomb to invoke her aid. Lucy and her mother spent the night in prayer outside of the tomb petitioning the saint for healing, as Lucy's

✠

mother suffered greatly from the ceaseless bleeding of a uterine hemorrhage. That night Agatha visited Lucy in a dream, telling her, "You have no need to invoke me, for your faith has already cured your mother. One day you will be known as the patron of your own city." As the day dawned, Lucy found her mother completely healed. She told her mother of her dream and confessed her secret vow of virginity. Impressed by Lucy's faith, her mother agreed not to force her into marriage.

Since she was no longer in need of a dowry, Lucy encouraged her mother to divest herself of all the investments she had made for her daughter's future and give the money to the poor. Lucy's fiancé, outraged to learn that their engagement was broken, denounced her faith to the governor of Siracusa. It was a dangerous time to be accused of following Christ. The emperor Diocletian had launched the most extensive and vicious anti-Christian campaign throughout the Roman Empire. When brought before the court to defend herself against the charges, Lucy asked, "Why would that man want to marry me?" The governor quipped, "Perhaps it is your lovely eyes." Lucy ripped out her eyeballs and told the governor to send them to her former fiancé. However, her eyesight was miraculously restored the next day, and she was again brought before the governor. He demanded why she so adamantly refused to marry. Lucy replied, "Those who live chaste lives are the temples of the Holy Spirit."

The governor then decreed that she be taken to a brothel and repeatedly raped until she "lost the Holy Spirit." Soldiers came to carry her off but could not move her. A thousand men were called in, to no avail. Lucy would not budge. Nor could a team of oxen drag her away. Burning pitch was poured on her skin but nothing would break her will. As she stood fast she predicted the fall of the emperor. Lucy was fatally stabbed in the throat for this pronouncement. True to her prophecy, the emperor fell within the year.

Immediately after her death, public opinion was so swayed by Lucy's fate that it was considered a great honor for other Christians to be buried near her in the catacombs of Siracusa. In the sixth century, the *Acts of the Virgin Martyrs* was given great recognition by ecclesiastical writers and Lucy's name was entered in the Canon of the Mass.

The people of her native city have always honored Lucy and been protective of her. In the ninth century when Siracusa fell into Muslim hands, faithful Christians hid Lucy's remains for hundreds of years until 1040, when the

"Those who live chaste lives are the temples of the Holy Spirit."

— Saint Lucy, A.D. 304

✝

Saint Lucy

Byzantine army drove out the Saracens. In gratitude for their liberation, they sent their most precious possession, her body, to Constantinople as a gift for the empress Theodora. Many of her relics were then distributed throughout Europe, which greatly expanded the range of her cult. In 1204, Venetian Crusaders conquered Constantinople and took Lucy's remains back to Venice, where they were installed in a church named for her. It happens that this original church was near the place where the gondolas were stored for the night. The song "Santa Lucia" became famous among gondoliers looking forward to the end of their night's work. When the church was later torn down to make way for a new train station, the station was named for Saint Lucy and her remains were interred in the nearby Church of Saint Jeremiah.

The name Lucy means light. According to the Julian calendar, her feast day, December 13, was considered the shortest day of the year. Celebrations combining Lucy's feast day with the winter solstice began in Sicily and spread throughout Europe. It was said that the "longest of nights and the shortest of days belong to Saint Lucy." Today, she is most celebrated in Sweden and other Scandinavian nations because when the Swedes converted to Christianity in the eleventh century, they could most easily relate to a saint who would gradually bring more light each day as the sun changed its course. Saint Lucy's Day is a major holiday in that part of the world, celebrated with torchlight processions of crowned girls in white dresses. With the change to the Gregorian calendar in the 1300s, and the shifting of the solstice to ten days later, Lucy's feast became synonymous with the start of the Christmas season. She is associated with gifts to children because of her part in curing an eye epidemic that caused blindness in children in the thirteenth century. When local families went on a barefoot pilgrimage to her tomb invoking her aid, she cured the children and sent them home, telling them that they would find gifts in their shoes. It became a common Christmas custom in many parts of Europe to celebrate the saint's feast by putting gifts in children's shoes. Lucy kept a careful watch over her native country as well, and, in 1582, Saint Lucy was credited with ending a famine in Sicily by sending three grain-loaded ships to its starving residents. The people were so hungry that they boiled and ate the grain without grinding it into flour. To this day, Sicilians do not eat anything made with flour on Saint Lucy's Day, and there are a host of traditional foods and desserts created specifically for her feast day.

54

Saint Lucy

Lucy is a popular subject for artists; she is frequently depicted calmly holding her eyeballs on a dish, referencing her story. Because of this, she is the patron of the blind and all trades relating to the eyes. Eye strain is a common problem for writers, therefore she is their patron. In art, she is sometimes portrayed in the company of saints Agatha, Agnes of Rome, Barbara, Thecla, and Catherine of Alexandria. All of them legendary young girls, defiant and fearless in the face of death. Because of her success in healing her mother, she is invoked against hemorrhage. Since she was stabbed in the throat, she protects against throat ailments and cutlers because she was killed by a knife. As a true patron of her city, Syracuse, she was historically called upon to help in all epidemics, hence her aid against dysentery. Peasants claim her patronage because they depend on oxen, which play a part in her rebellion against the governor. Her final resting place is Venice, so she is also known as the patron of that city's glaziers and gondoliers.

Prayer to Saint Lucy of Syracuse
Saint Lucy, your beautiful name signifies light.
By the light of faith which God bestowed upon you,
Increase and preserve this light in my soul so that I may avoid evil,
Be zealous in the performance of good works,
and abhor nothing as much as the blindness and darkness of
  evil and sin.
By your intercession with God,
obtain for me perfect vision for my bodily eyes
and the grace to use them for God's greater honor and glory
and the salvation of all men.
Saint Lucy, virgin and martyr,
Hear my prayers and obtain my petitions.
Amen.

☩

Saint Lucy

A.D. 270–345

Saint Nicholas

Feast Day: December 6
Patron of: Apulia, Bari, Greece, Italy, the Kingdom of Naples, Russia, Sicily, apothecaries, bakers, barrel makers, boatmen, butchers, children, dockworkers, grain vendors, murderers, paupers, pawnbrokers, pharmacists, thieves, wine vendors, the wrongfully accused
Invoked for: happy marriages blessed with children
Invoked against: judicial error
Symbols: anchor, bishop's staff, miter, ship, three bags of money, three gold balls

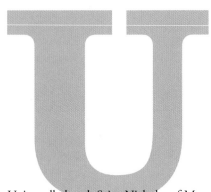

Universally loved, Saint Nicholas of Myra is so revered in the East that he is invoked in the Orthodox Mass. In the West, he has come to symbolize the celebration of Christmas in the form of a character named Santa Claus, or St. Nick. The traditions of Christmas reflect his life of wonders, which began in Patara, Turkey. As a wealthy young orphan, Nicholas had great compassion for the poor and freely shared his inheritance with others. When he heard that one of his neighbors was so desperately impoverished he was considering selling his three daughters into prostitution, Nicholas secretly went to the man's house on three consecutive nights. Each night, he threw a bag of gold coins through an open window, providing a dowry for the girls and sparing them a horrible fate.

Compassion and care for others, regardless of their circumstances, were prevailing traits throughout Saint Nicholas's life. When the local governor took a bribe to execute three innocent men, Nicholas boldly stayed the hand of the executioner and ordered the men freed. He then reproached the governor until the man admitted his crime and repented for it publicly. Three Roman officers who had witnessed this event were later wrongfully arrested and ordered executed in Constantinople. They appealed to God to send Nicholas to help them win their freedom. That night both the emperor Constantine and the local prefect had dreams of Nicholas berating them. When they compared notes the next morning, they sent for the condemned men, who told them of their appeal to Nicholas, who was by then the bishop of Myra. Constantine then freed the men and sent them to Nicholas with a letter asking him not to threaten him anymore but to pray for the peace of the world.

Even in his own lifetime, Nicholas was considered a saint, having received

‡

Saint Nicholas

"The West as the East acclaims and glorifies him. Wherever there are people, in the country and the town, in the villages, in the isles, in the furthest parts of the earth, his name is revered and churches are built in his honor. Images of him are set up, panegyrics preached and festivals celebrated. All Christians young and old, men and women, boys and girls, reverence his memory and call upon his protection. And his favors, which know no limit of time and continue from age to age, are poured out all over the earth; the Scythians know them, as do the Indians and the barbarians, the Africans as well as the Italians."

— anonymous Greek, tenth century A.D.

‡

Saint Nicholas

the bishopric of Myra under supernatural circumstance. At the time, the sea-coast capital's bishop died suddenly, and the Christian community was at a loss for his successor. A neighboring bishop was told in a dream to name the first man who entered the church the next morning their new bishop. Nicholas was visiting the city and happened to enter the church at dawn's first light. He was thus embraced and consecrated as bishop of Myra. He accepted his office with grace and humility, standing fast against the persecutions of Diocletian, the Roman emperor. As bishop, Nicholas was said to be present at the Council of Nicaea in 325. There, he defended the teachings of the Holy Trinity against Arius, who argued against the divinity of Christ. For his holy stance, he was thrown into prison; however, Christ and the Virgin Mary appeared to him and restored his robes and holy office. Once free, he single-handedly brought down the megalithic Temple of Diana (the Greek goddess Artemis). According to legend, screaming demons fled as the great stones fell. Ironically, December 6, the feast day of Saint Nicholas, was also the day once celebrated as Diana's birthday.

Besides his love for justice, Nicholas was known as a loving shepherd of his people. During a famine that threatened his region, he heard there were ships in the harbor filled with grain. He went to the boats and asked the sailors for one hundred bushels. The grain had been carefully measured for the city of Alexandria and the sailors were terrified to deliver it with any shortages. Nicholas convinced them to give a little bit from each boat, assuring them that the customs officer would never know the difference. The grain he obtained lasted for two years, successfully ending the famine. True to his word, the sailors' donation went undetected.

Though he is the patron of children, one of the only stories of Saint Nicholas and children is a grim one. A butcher abducted three young boys to make into bacon. After cutting them up he packed them in a barrel of brine to cure. The boys' location was revealed to Nicholas in a dream. He went to the butcher and demanded to see the barrel, then miraculously pulled three

‡

Saint Nicholas

whole boys from it, restoring them to life. The butcher confessed and repented for his crime. Because of this, Nicholas is the patron of butchers, barrel makers, and murderers.

There are several stories of people borrowing money and swearing on an altar of Saint Nicholas to repay it. In one, a liar insists he had already paid his debt. While leaving the convinced court, he gloated at his moneylender. On his way home, however, he was killed in an accident on the road. The money he falsely claimed to have paid spilled out from its hiding place in his cane. Instead of picking up the money, which was rightfully his, the moneylender first invoked Saint Nicholas to bring the man back to life. Only after the liar was breathing again and able to stand up did the moneylender pick up the coins–converting to Christianity as the liar repented.

Since Myra is on the coast, there are many tales of Nicholas helping sailors at sea. He would appear to them in dreams, advising them how to steer through rough passages. "May Saint Nicholas hold the tiller," is a common good luck saying among sailors on the Aegean and Ionian seas. Sailors spread tales of his wonder working in every port they entered. For this reason, there are numerous seaport chapels dedicated to Saint Nicholas. Before the Reformation, England alone had over four hundred churches in his name. When Myra fell under Muslim rule, sailors from Bari, Italy, posed as visiting pilgrims and stole the saint's remains. With the monks and townspeople of Myra in hot pursuit, they carried Nicholas's bones back to Bari, where they built a magnificent cathedral to house them. This is still a major pilgrimage site in Christendom, particularly for women having trouble conceiving children. On May 9, the feast of the translation of Nicholas's remains, manna, or sacred oil with healing powers, is extracted from his bones, diluted, and stored in hand-painted bottles. Bari is filled with pilgrims from both the East and the West who travel great distances to celebrate this festival. Many come from Russia where his cult was introduced in the eleventh century by Vladmir I. Nicholas is still invoked there as a protector

✝

Saint Nicholas

of the oppressed and poor. His great popularity in Germany goes back even further, stemming from the devotion of the Greek wife of the emperor in the eighth century.

Because of his practice of anonymous generosity, the French would honor Nicholas by leaving gifts and candy to poor children on December 5, Saint Nicholas's Eve. This custom was taken up all over Western Europe but particularly embraced in the Netherlands. After the Reformation, when honoring saints became suspect, Martin Luther moved the customary celebration of Saint Nicholas's Day to December 25, changing it into a celebration of the birth of Christ. However, Saint Nicholas lived on in the common people in the guise of Sinta Klaus (Saint Claus). The first Dutch settlers in New York brought their traditional celebration of Saint Nicholas with them, while German immigrants made Christmas a major celebration. The image of Saint Nicholas driving a sled with reindeer was taken from the German myths of the gods. Odin was said to fly through the heavens the same way. In the early 1800s, visual depictions of Saint Nicholas evolved from an iconic Eastern bishop with a beard to a jolly Dutch burgher. Publication of the poem "A Visit from St. Nicholas" ("The Night Before Christmas") in 1823 completed his transformation from the wonder-working fourth-century saint to our present-day popular figure of Santa Claus.

One need only look at the extensive list of his patronage (only a fraction of which is listed above) to see how immensely popular this saint is. Since Saint Nicholas was a defender of the Holy Trinity, tales of his wonder working frequently feature three individuals or three objects. It is said when he rescued his neighbor's daughters that the three bags of gold landed in stockings hung to dry over the fireplace. This is where we get our tradition of Christmas stockings. Oranges or chocolate-covered gold coins also signify these bags of gold. Candy canes are symbols of his bishop's staff.

Vintage card

‡

Saint Nicholas

Because of his defense of the wronged moneylender–a reviled profession in ancient times–pawnbrokers adopted him as a patron and use as their symbol the three golden balls. Thieves and murderers also claim his patronage, citing his sincere forgiveness of them following their repentance. Nicholas is also invoked for helping the wrongly accused to receive justice. His patronage of children stems from bringing the three murdered boys back to life, and his patronage of bakers and grain sellers is derived from his saving the city of Myra during the famine. In art, Saint Nicholas is always depicted with a beard, a bishop's hat, and staff, usually with three objects or three figures from the tales of his wonder working.

Eastern Orthodox Saint Nicholas Prayer
Almighty God, who in your love gave to your servant
Nicholas of Myra
a perpetual name for deeds of kindness on land and sea:
Grant, we pray, that your Church may never cease to
work for the happiness of children,
the safety of sailors,
the relief of the poor,
and the help of those tossed by tempests of doubt
or grief;
through Jesus Christ our Lord,
who lives and reigns with you and the Holy Spirit,
One God, for ever and ever.
Amen.

✝

Saint Nicholas

FOURTH CENTURY

Saint Ursula

Feast Day: October 21
Patron of: British Virgin Islands; Cologne, Germany; University of Paris; archers, drapers, educators, girls, orphans
Invoked for: the education of girls and women, a happy marriage, a holy death
Invoked against: shipwrecks on rivers
Symbols: arrows, cloak, crown, pilgrim's staff with white flag and red cross, ship

ESSENDO: CA
MERAR: I
MAGISTRO

The story of Saint Ursula and her army of eleven thousand virgins was a major influence on the creative world of the Middle Ages and the Renaissance. The tale made a fascinating subject for artists of all disciplines, and the early Middle Ages are filled with accounts of mystics communicating with the souls of the young maidens. Images of thousands of girls fearlessly sailing around in their own ships captured the popular imagination. Their tragic and daring tale of martyrdom inspired one of the finest pieces of liturgical music ever written, "Chants for the Feast of Saint Ursula," and the artists Caravaggio, Giovanni Bellini, and Claude Lorrain have all celebrated her as a famous subject. Almost every country of Europe has an artistically important visual rendition of Ursula's story. The Reliquary of Saint Ursula can be found in Bruges and is said to contain an arm of the saint. It is adorned with six miniatures by Hans Memling. The Scuola di San' Orsola in Venice commissioned the artist Carpaccio to create his greatest work, *The Dream of Saint Ursula,* a series of paintings based on the life of the saint, which tell her story in an almost cinematic way.

There are many different versions of this story, the first known one appearing in the eighth century when the Cult of Saint Ursula was strong. The authenticity of her legend is based on ten lines carved in the late fifth century, now found in the Church of Saint Ursula at Cologne, Germany. The words were written by a senator named Clematius who attests that due to a spiritual vision, he is dedicating a church on the grounds of an older basilica built to honor the virgins of Cologne martyred on that site on October 21 a century earlier.

The first written accounts of her martyrdom come a century later and nearly five hundred years after her death. They depict Ursula as the Christian

‡

Saint Ursula

daughter of a British king who, in order to avoid a war, agrees to an arranged marriage to a pagan prince. On the advice of an angel received in a dream, Ursula requested that she travel for three years, visiting the holy shrines of the Christians. She would bring with her ten noblewomen who would each be accompanied by one thousand virgin companions. So great was Ursula's beauty that the neighboring king and his son readily agreed to her request. They helped amass the eleven thousand virgins from kingdoms all over the known world. Men being unwelcome on such a voyage, Ursula and her virgins were trained in sailing their eleven massive ships, which first sailed to Cologne, Germany, and then on to Basel, where the women proceeded on foot through the Alps down to Rome. Gradually, these accompanying maidens converted from their pagan faiths to Christianity, and they were given a joyous reception by the pope and the Christian community. On their return voyage, they stopped again at Cologne, which had been over-run by the Huns. The invaders hated the prospect of so many future Christian mothers taking over the continent and the virgins were massacred. Ursula was spared for her beauty, and the leader of the Huns demanded that she marry him. When she refused, he shot her in the chest with an arrow. After her death, an army of eleven thousand angels chased the Huns from Cologne, and the grateful population converted to Christianity and erected a basilica in honor of Ursula and her virgins.

It is thought the very early stories of the virgin martyrs actually only included eleven young women, Ursula being one of them. As the tale was recorded in Latin, the number eleven was transposed into eleven thousand, making the original story more fantastic with each recounting. In mythology, Urschel is also the name of the Teutonic moon goddess who welcomed the souls of dead maidens. It is thought that the history of this early virgin martyr could have been confused and combined with the legend of this goddess who also sailed up the Rhine River with a boatload of virginal companions.

"For this most chaste and golden army crossed the sea with maidenly, flowing hair. O who has ever heard such great things?"

— from "Chants for the Feast of Saint Ursula"
by Hildegarde von Bingen, twelfth century

☦

Saint Ursula

It is in Ursula's influence on a woman who lived a thousand years after her death that we feel her impact in modern times. In the sixteenth century, the Italian saint Angela Merici was inspired by her own personal visions of Saint Ursula and her virgins to found an order of nuns dedicated to educating young women. This was considered a revolutionary concept at a time when women were scarcely allowed to leave their homes. These were the first schools established for girls and young women in Europe, later coming to the Americas in the seventeenth century. Today, Ursuline academies and colleges take seriously their mandate to educate young women throughout the world, and this order of teaching nuns maintains Saint Ursula as their patron.

Chapel of the Ursuline nuns, Quebec

✝

Saint Ursula

Though her cult is most popular in Germany and Eastern Europe, Saint Ursula can be found on the flag of the British Virgin Islands where her feast day, October 21, is a national holiday. The islands were discovered by Columbus on his second voyage in 1493. He named a larger island Saint Ursula and the surrounding ones Once Mil Virgines (Eleven Thousand Virgins). Eventually, this name was shortened to the Virgin Islands, which is what they are known as today. Her iconography reflects the events of her life. Since Ursula was a British princess, she is depicted with a crown, and the flag she carries is the banner of Saint George, the Christian flag of England. She is frequently sheltering young girls under a cloak, and for this reason she is the patron saint of drapers. Because her fiancé was so agreeable to granting her request to travel, she is invoked for happy marriages. She was martyred by an arrow, so she is the patron saint of archers. Today, Saint Ursula is most associated with the education and empowerment of young girls.

Prayer to Saint Ursula
By the merits of our Lord Jesus Christ, accept, O God,
The prayers offered to you through the intercession of Saint Ursula,
Faithful imitator of the virtues of the Heart of your Son,
And grant us the favors we are confidently asking for. Amen.
Saint Ursula, pray for us!
Amen.

Saint Ursula

A.D. 480–547

Saint Benedict
Abbot and Founder of the Benedictine Order

Feast Day: July 11
Patron of: Europe, architects, chemists, coppersmiths, the dying
engineers, farmers, monks, those in religious orders, schoolchildren,
speleologists
Invoked against: gallstones, gossip, inflammatory diseases,
kidney diseases, poisoning, temptation
Symbols: book of the Rule, broken sieve, cup with two serpents,
miter, pastoral staff, raven with bread in its beak

Though his sole intention was the moral and spiritual training of individuals seeking a holy life, Saint Benedict is credited with saving Western civilization during the Dark Ages. Benedictine builders and architects created cathedrals, abbeys, castles, and churches in every country of Europe. Regions scattered throughout the continent owe their agricultural prosperity to the skills of Benedictine monks in reviving lost farming practices. Because of this Order, ancient literature was preserved, pioneering strides in medicine were made, and schools and universities were created that still exist today. After 1,500 years, the Benedictine Rule is the basis of all Western monastic rules and for this reason Benedict is considered the patriarch of Western religious orders.

Most of what is known about the life of Saint Benedict comes from the *Dialogues of Gregory the Great.* Those consulted for these writings included Benedict's first followers and eyewitnesses to his life. *The Dialogues* was completed within a generation of his death.

According to this history, Benedict and his twin sister, Scholastica, were born in Nursia (today's Norcia), a prosperous town in Umbria. His family sent him to Rome to complete his higher education. He was appalled to find that a study of rhetoric had replaced the search for truth, and that his fellow students seemed to squander every one of their advantages in the pursuit of pleasure. Disgusted by the corruption in the government and the schisms in the Church, Benedict gave up his inheritance and went off to live forty miles away in the city of Affile. There he began studying the Bible with a small group of like-minded young men. His diligence was rewarded one day when his servant accidentally broke a wheat sifter. Benedict picked up the pieces to examine them and the sifter was miraculously made whole. The notoriety of his first miracle forced him to go into hiding. This time he moved into a

✝

Saint Benedict

cave on the ridge of Mount Subiaco. A hermit living nearby advised him and brought him food. Benedict spent three years there, praying and studying. The devil appeared to him as a blackbird that constantly circled his face. When Benedict made the sign of the cross, it disappeared but he was instantly seized with an attack of lust for a woman he had previously known. He threw off his tunic and rolled himself in the sharp nettles and brambles to stop his thoughts, ridding himself of further temptation.

Benedict's reputation for holiness spread, and the monks of Viscovo asked him to be their leader. He warned them that he would be too strict an authority for them, but they insisted that he come. When Benedict's prediction proved true, they tried to put poison in his wine to get rid of him. However, he made the sign of the cross over the cup and it shattered. Benedict forgave the monks and returned to his cave.

As his fame spread, many came to Subiaco asking for guidance in living a monastic life. At that time, the first monastic communities had been formed in the East, and they included harsh ascetic deprivations that Benedict felt served to hinder a true study of scripture. As an alternative, he set up twelve religious houses of twelve men each, with their own patriarch. He lived in a thirteenth house, with several other monks in training. When he realized that it was a major problem for his monks to bring fresh water up the mountains on a daily basis, Benedict spent the night in prayer. At dawn, a natural spring appeared, capable of supplying water to all thirteen communities. It is still in existence today.

These and other little miracles became well known to the surrounding towns. Many looked to this religious community of laymen for their spiritual guidance, and the local priest was overcome with jealousy. As a legitimate member of the clergy, it infuriated him that he did not warrant half the respect of Benedict and his followers. When the priest tried to poison Benedict with a loaf of bread, a raven snatched it out of Benedict's hands and flew off with it. This raven frequently appears in Benedict's iconography, along with the cup of poisoned wine wrapped in serpents, which symbolize the devil.

Religious counsel was only one area in which the Benedictines served their neighbors. They developed farming techniques that greatly improved the fortunes of those toiling in the fields. And because of their reputation for higher learning, these same local people entreated the monks to start a school. Students came from far-off places to study with these learned men. While Benedict was meeting with a monk named Maurus, he had a vision of a student named Placidus drowning in a lake. He ordered Maurus to save the

"Pray and Work."

— a summation of the Rule of Saint Benedict

✠

Saint Benedict

child. Only after he had safely gotten the boy ashore did Maurus realize that he had actually run across the surface of the lake to do so. Benedict's ability to see multiple things happening at one time would continue over his lifetime.

Placidus came from a wealthy family and in gratitude for saving his son's life, his father gave Benedict the citadel of Monte Cassino. Located high up on a mountain ridge, Monte Cassino had stood as a shrine to the gods Apollo and Jove. After spending forty days in prayer, Benedict cut down the grove of trees sacred to the gods. On the place of the temple to Jupiter, he built a church named for Saint Martin and another named for Saint John the Baptist, considered the ideal hermit. Instead of having many small houses of monks, Benedict decided to have one large one, and in 530 the building of the most famous monastery in the world began.

The monastery at Monte Cassino was built as a city of God. Benedict was not a priest and his followers were not educated clergymen but laymen who wanted to live good lives as proscribed in the Gospel. Benedict wrote out a Rule, which every Western monastery since has based its founding principles on. This Rule was a startling break from the ideas of the day. As written, all monks had to work, either in the fields or in the construction of buildings. All monks were equal regardless of the social level into which they were born. All monks would spend hours a day reading. Prayer was to consist of the Psalms and Canticles, with the entire Psalter being recited within a week. The Rule did not legislate private prayer but advised it to be short and heartfelt. Excessive self-deprivation was discouraged, as it was often a form of vanity. Benedict's order of monks was also encouraged to have as much food and wine as needed, as well as warm blankets and clothing. They ate no meat from four-legged creatures and remained celibate. Hospitality was to be granted to all travelers, and any visitor who was willing to follow the laws of the monastery could stay as long as he or she wanted. The Rule also outlined

74

✝

Saint Benedict

the responsibility of the monastery to help the surrounding community in any way possible. This included sharing food, crops, and helping with repayment of debt. By having a Rule to follow, it became possible for other religious orders to model their communities after the great monastery at Monte Cassino. Though the Rule is written for men, it proved to be an equally effective model for women's convents.

Near the end of his life, Benedict was outdoors in the middle of the night when a single ray of the sun appeared, illuminating the entire universe. He believed he had actually seen God and considered this the greatest of all his earthly experiences. When his sister Scholastica met him in the little house she kept outside the gates of the monastery for their yearly visit, she asked him to stay the night. He told her it was impossible to leave his duties. She bowed her head in prayer as he was leaving and a fierce thunderstorm erupted, forcing Benedict to stay. She told him that she asked God for that which Benedict refused, and God granted her prayer. Brother and sister spent the night talking and reminiscing before he returned to the monastery. Three days later, Benedict saw a dove fly into the sky. He realized it was the soul of Scholastica on its way to heaven and knew his own death would soon follow. Having the gift of prophecy, he had his tomb opened and spent six days in prayer. He fell into a high fever and died surrounded by his followers.

Though Benedict never traveled out of Monte Cassino, at one time there were over forty thousand monasteries following his rule. His system of constant work and study created great prosperity in the areas surrounding the monasteries that employed it. While chaos and instability plunged Europe into the Dark Ages, the Benedictine monasteries were enlightened places where knowledge was preserved and shared. The immense monastery of Monte Cassino was completely destroyed in one of the fiercest battles of the Second World War, and the only parts of it not obliterated were the underground cell of Benedict, his tomb, and that of his sister.

✝

Saint Benedict

In art, Benedict is traditionally depicted with an open book of his Rule, usually inscribed with "Pray and Work." At times a cup wrapped in two serpents is near him, symbolizing the attempts to poison him. In many instances the raven who saved him is also with him. The raven is also a symbol of the hermit, since this bird was credited with dropping food to the original desert fathers. Benedict's patronage extends to engineers, architects, and farmers because of the advances made in those fields by the early Benedictine monks. His early schools make him the patron of schoolchildren. He is invoked against kidney ailments and kidney stones because of his powers to heal them. Because he was a victim, of diabolic temptations, gossipmongers, and poisoners, he is also called on for protection against these situations. Because he could predict the time of his own and others' deaths, he is invoked by the dying for a good death.

Prayer to Saint Benedict

O glorious Saint Benedict, sublime model of all virtues, pure vessel of God's grace!
Behold me, humbly kneeling at thy feet.
I implore thy loving heart to pray for me before the throne of God.
To thee I have recourse in all dangers which daily surround me.
Shield me against my enemies, inspire me to imitate thee in all things.
May thy blessing be with thee always, so that I may shun whatever God forbids and avoid the occasions of sin.
Graciously obtain for me from God those favors and graces of which I stand so much in need, in the trials, miseries, and afflictions of life.
Thy heart was always so full of love, compassion, and mercy
towards those who were afflicted or troubled in any way.
Thou didst never dismiss without consolation and assistance anyone who had recourse to thee.
I therefore invoke they powerful intercession,
in the confident hope that thou will hear my prayers
and obtain for me the special grace and favor I so earnestly implore
[mention], and if it be for the greater glory of God and the welfare
of my soul.
Help me, O great Saint Benedict, to live and die as a faithful child of God,
to be ever submissive to His holy will, and to attain the eternal happiness of heaven.
Amen.

‡

saints

1182–1226

Saint Francis of Assisi
Founder of the Franciscan Order: Friars Minor,
the Poor Clares, the Third Order of Saint Francis

Feast Day: October 4
Patron of: Italy, San Francisco, animals, ecology, merchants,
nature, peace, tapestry workers
Invoked for: harmony
Invoked against: dying alone
Symbols: communing with crucifix, preaching to birds,
receiving stigmata

Reviled, ridiculed, and considered a raving madman by his contemporaries, Francis of Assisi turned his back on the comfortable world of his birth to revitalize the message of Christ. By the time of his death, his holiness was universally recognized and he had shaken the staid convictions of church and political officials to their core. Today, his simple message of love for God, the earth, and all its creatures makes him revered by Catholics and non-Catholics alike.

Born Giovanni Bernadone in the prosperous hill town of Assisi, he was a spoiled and indulged young man given to dressing well, playing pranks, and carousing with friends. The son of a wealthy cloth merchant, he was nicknamed Francesco ("The Frenchman") because of his French mother. On a boastful lark at the age of twenty, he fought in a minor war against the neighboring town of Perugia. Everything changed when the enemy captured him and he spent a year in prison. When his father finally ransomed him home, Francis was ill with malaria and debilitated. Forced to endure months of quiet bed rest in order to recover, he found it hard to resume his old ways. Neither his friends nor his father's business held much interest for him.

In an effort to regain his former life, Francis made an attempt to fight for the Papal States under Walter de Brienne. Equipped with the finest armor, he met a shabbily clad knight along the way and on a whim exchanged clothes with him. That night in a dream, a voice told him to turn back and serve "the Master rather than the man." After his father and friends ridiculed him for his desertion, he roamed the countryside alone in a state of spiritual crisis. One day, as he was wandering, Francis came upon a leper and was initially revolted by his sores. However, instead of turning away, Francis leapt from his horse, gave the leper all his money, and then kissed his hand. Thus began

‡

Saint Francis of Assisi

what Francis later called his conversion. It also began his daily ritual of visiting hospitals and leper colonies and meditating in the crumbling church of San Damiano.

Just beyond the walls of Assisi, San Damiano had been deserted by the town's faithful and was tended by a single elderly priest. In 1205, while Francis was praying in front of the crucifix, he heard a voice, "Go, Francis, and repair my house which as you see, is falling into ruin." Looking around at the decaying structure, Francis interpreted this request literally. He hurried to his father's shop, bundled up as much fabric and drapery as he could carry, and sold it in the marketplace in order to buy building supplies. His father was furious and dragged him to the city consuls, not only to recover the money for the fabric but to force Francis to denounce his inheritance as well. At this meeting, Francis insisted that he was a servant of God and should not be judged by a civil court. He relinquished the gold and stripped himself of all his belongings. Handing them to his father he said, "From now onwards, I can turn to God and call him my father in heaven!" He left Assisi dressed in the garments of a hermit.

Although he was now penniless, Francis was still intent on keeping his promise to rebuild San Damiano. He begged for stones and alms in the street, and the townfolk considered him a madman. He did eventually complete his task and Francis went on to repair other churches, including Santa Maria degli Angeli, known as the Porziuncola. Considered by Francis to be "one of the holiest places on earth," this little chapel was originally erected in 353 by hermits from the Valley of Josaphat. It housed relics of the Virgin Mary and became known as Our Lady of the Angels because people reported hearing the sound of singing angels coming from inside at night. Francis, who had a deep connection to the Virgin Mary, built himself a hut near her church and would pray for her intercession in giving him earthly direction. On February 24, 1209, while at mass, he heard the Gospel of Matthew 10:9, where Jesus told his followers, "And going, preach, saying The Kingdom of Heaven is at hand . . . Freely have you received. Freely give. Take neither gold nor silver nor brass in your purses . . . nor two coats, nor shoes nor a staff . . . Behold I send you forth as sheep in the midst of wolves . . ."

Stricken to the core, Francis immediately cast off what few possessions he

"Go, Francis, and repair my house which, as you see, is falling into ruin."

— from the crucifix on the crumbling wall of San Damiano

✝

Saint Francis of Assisi

had until he was dressed only in the coarse woolen tunic of the poor. He set out to Assisi to preach penance, brotherly love, and peace. His manner was so warm and sincere that, instead of scoffing at him, people listened with fascination to what he had to say. Here before them was the most Christlike man they had ever seen. The Porziuncola filled with his followers. By the end of that year, a small community of eleven men was following Francis and the simple Rule he wrote adapting the precepts of the gospel.

In the summer of 1210, Francis and his companions traveled to Rome to seek the blessing of the pope for this new order of Friars Minor. Papal ecclesiastical advisers declared that the Rule of the Order, though taken solely from Christ's command, was impractical and unsafe, and Francis's request was rejected. That night Pope Innocent III had a dream in which Francis was holding up the Lateran Church with his shoulder. The next morning the pope immediately requested an audience with Francis and approved his mission. Upon the Friars' return to Umbria, the Benedictine Order attempted to give them the Porziuncola for their monastery. Francis only accepted the use of the property. He strongly felt that their Order must always live in holy poverty, never owning anything. Even their name, Friars Minor (Little Brothers) reminded the men to never exalt themselves above anyone.

The first Friars Minor traveled throughout Italy, joyfully preaching by day and sleeping in haylofts at night. Forbidden to take money, they supported their mission by working with laborers in the fields or begging for their meals. Having proved themselves adept at local peacemaking and sowing contentment, many of the Italian city-states invited them to preach and set up small communities within their borders. Missions were sent to Spain, Germany, Hungary, and France. Without trying to be revolutionaries, Francis and his

✠

Saint Francis of Assisi

followers completely changed the way the Church reached people. Because he truly believed that all of nature was wondrous and all creatures sacred to God, Francis introduced a new way of looking at the world, one accessible to rich and poor alike. His order attracted a socially diverse group of men and spawned an affiliated women's order with Saint Clare of Assisi. He later drew up a rule for laity who desired to associate themselves with the Friars Minor. This order of Franciscan Tertiaries, or the Third Order of Saint Francis, exists today with worldwide membership from the Catholic, Episcopal, and Anglican Churches. Just as they did under Francis, members continue to follow the rules of humility, charity, and voluntary poverty.

Francis was a true mystic. It was said that birds would quiet down and listen when he preached, and there are many tales of his ability to communicate with animals. When the citizens of Gubbio were being terrorized by a man-eating wolf, for example, Francis went up in the hills to find it. Upon seeing the vicious animal, he made the sign of the cross and invited the wolf to come to him. The wolf docilely lay at his feet, and Francis drafted a pact between the wolf and the citizens of Gubbio; in exchange for being regularly fed by the town, the wolf would leave its residents in peace. Both sides agreed, and Gubbio was freed from this menace.

Francis's life of sacrifice and self-deprivation put an incredible strain on his body. When he prayed, the light he saw in his raptures was so intense that it caused him to continuously weep. His followers feared for his eyesight, but he said he could not resist being in the presence of such a brilliant light. His devotions became more and more extreme and in August of 1224 Francis retired to the secluded mountain of La Verna for a forty-day retreat before the Feast of Saint Michael. He devoted most of his meditations to the wounds

‡

Saint Francis of Assisi

and suffering of Christ. At dawn on September 14, after a night of prayer, he had a vision of a Seraphim angel, nailed to a cross, flying at him. When the vision vanished, his body bore the stigmata of the crucified Christ. He bore these markings in secrecy for the last two years of his life. They were visible upon his death in October 1226.

The contributions of Francis of Assisi were not limited to religion. A great writer and poet, he wrote "Canticle of the Sun," his masterpiece inspired by Saint Clare, in his native Italian. Writing in a language other than Latin was uncommon at the time, and it set the groundwork for the poetry of Dante Aligheri, a great admirer of Francis. Publicly acclaimed as a saint in his own lifetime, Francis of Assisi led one of the most documented lives of the Middle Ages. Within decades of his death, there were numerous biographies written by his followers. Perhaps the greatest memorial to this saint is the Basilica of Saint Francis, commissioned by the city of Assisi two years after his death. Considered one of the most important monuments of Europe, Giotto, Cimabue, and Simone Martini, the greatest artists of their day, decorated the interior with scenes from the saint's life. Assisi itself exudes such an air of peace and love from having the presence of such a graceful being in its midst that it remains an important site for pilgrims devoted to the memory and teachings of Il Poverello ("The Little Poor Man") known as Saint Francis.

Stigmatization of Saint Francis

✠

Saint Francis of Assisi

Because of his extensive travels through Italy, his great love of his native land, and his important writings in Italian, Saint Francis is the patron saint of Italy. He is the patron of merchants and tapestry workers because of his father's business. Since he is best known as one who lived in and greatly loved nature and all creatures, he is the patron of ecology, animals, and nature. In art, he is depicted conversing with animals, sometimes with the wolf of Gubbio, most often with birds or receiving the stigmata. In 1223, Francis invented the Christmas manger, today a common sight in Catholic homes and churches.

Blessing of Saint Francis of Assisi
May the Lord bless you
and keep you;
may the Lord show his face to you
and have compassion on you!
May he turn his face to you
and give you peace!
Amen.

87

✠

Saint Francis of Assisi

1193–1254

Saint Clare of Assisi
Abbess and Founder of the Poor Clares

Feast Day: August 11
Patron of: embroiderers, eye disease, gilders, goldsmiths, laundry workers, oculists, telephones, television
Invoked for: good sight
Invoked against: fever, blindness
Symbols: cross, lamp, lily, monstrance, olive branch

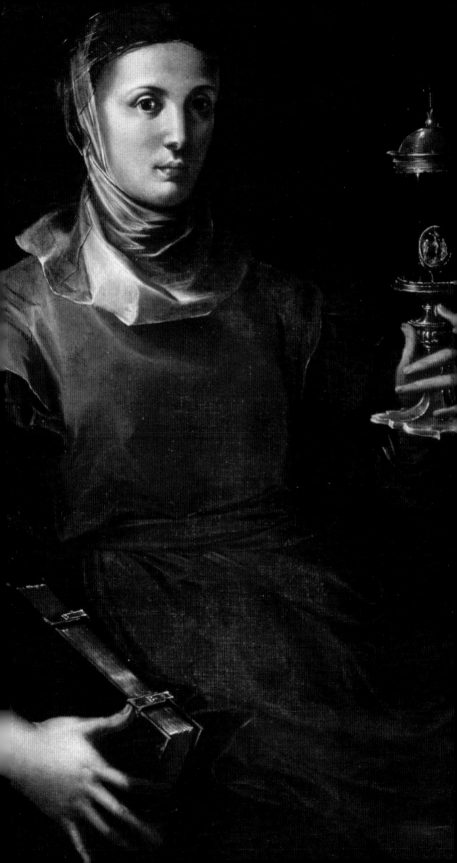

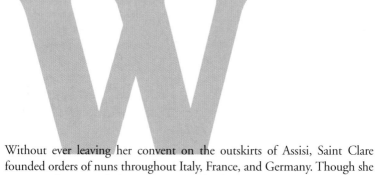

Without ever leaving her convent on the outskirts of Assisi, Saint Clare founded orders of nuns throughout Italy, France, and Germany. Though she maintained a vow of silence, popes, cardinals, and royalty came to her for spiritual advice. Only twelve years younger than her mentor, Saint Francis of Assisi, she quietly helped him lead a movement of young people that con-

fronted the church hierarchy for their material excesses, and revolutionized religious expression by embracing simplicity and poverty.

Chiara Offreduccio was the daughter of a wealthy count and countess in Assisi, Italy, and displayed little interest in the worldly advantages offered by her highborn state. She was eighteen and destined for an arranged, profitable marriage when she heard Saint Francis deliver the Lenten sermon at her church. Inspired by his simple message of living with complete trust in God, she conspired to run away and live like this new order of mendicant friars, dependent solely on alms received from begging. The turning point for her occurred on Palm Sunday, 1212. On that day, Clare went to the Cathedral of Assisi in her finest clothes for the blessing of the palms. While others went to the altar rail to receive their palms, she sat in her seat, too shy to move. With the entire congregation as witness, the bishop stepped down from the altar and delivered the palms to her. She took this as a sign to act on her plan.

Homes in Assisi were built with two doors, one for regular use and one called the Door of the Dead, opened only to remove a coffin from the house. That night, Clare secretly cleared the debris from the Door of the Dead and stepped through it, renouncing her former life and the material world forever. She slipped through the woods to the chapel of the Porziuncola, where Francis and his small community of men were at prayer. Clare exchanged her finery for a penitential tunic of coarse cloth tied with a rope, and Francis cut off her

‡

Saint Clare of Assisi

luxurious hair in front of the Blessed Virgin's altar. Having no separate living facility for women, he then took her to the local Benedictine convent.

Clare's family embarked on a rescue mission, sparing no expense. During a violent struggle to drag Clare from the convent, her clothing was torn off, and her shorn hair revealed. She declared to her shocked father, "The only spouse I will have is Christ, and further attempts to remove me from my chosen life will make me more steadfast!" Her powerful father had to submit to her will and leave her behind. To his great anguish his younger daughter Agnes joined Clare just two weeks later. Thus began a fashionable tradition of wealthy young women turning their backs on privilege and society in order to follow a higher spiritual path. Francis of Assisi had offered his peers a way of living that shook the foundations of society in the Middle Ages. Instead of becoming dependent behind the walls of staid, established religious orders, he encouraged his followers to exist in a day-to-day manner, experiencing nature and depending on the goodwill of others. The joy he and his band of friars exuded was infectious and he developed a following wherever he went. Clare was the first young woman with the courage to join him.

In 1215, when Clare was twenty-two years old, Saint Francis installed her as the Abbess of the Order of Poor Ladies in a small house across from the Church of San Damiano. These women followed the Franciscan rule, forbidden to own property or material goods and entirely dependent on the alms the Friars Minor could beg for them. Upon the death of her father, Clare did not veer from Saint Francis's teachings. She gave her vast inheritance to the poor rather than to her own religious community. This act of devotion caused much controversy–Church authorities expected women to give their dowries to the religious orders they joined. This was to ensure that the nuns would be supported throughout their lives and would not serve as a burden to their parish communities. Because she was the founder of this order of women, Clare set a precedent for future Franciscan convents.

Despite this disagreement with church hierarchy, convents of Poor Clares, as the order became known, were started in cities all over Italy, gradually spreading to France and Germany. These first convents attracted many educated and wealthy women who not only walked away from titles and estates but also lived in a state of self-imposed austerity that was considered extreme for men and unheard of for women. They went barefoot, wore sackcloth, slept on the ground, ate no meat, and maintained a vow of silence, speaking only out of necessity. Agnes, daughter of the King of Bohemia, broke her

"Love God, serve God: Everything is in that."

— Clare of Assisi

‡

Saint Clare of Assisi

engagement to become empress of the Holy Roman Empire to start an order of Poor Clares. The correspondence between Agnes and Clare leaves a lasting portrayal of the intellectual brilliance and good nature of the order's founder.

Because of her great mind, Saint Clare was an invaluable adviser to Saint Francis. When he was wrestling with the choice of becoming a religious hermit or going out in the world to evangelize his movement, she encouraged him to go out to the people. It was Clare who nursed Francis through the last days of his life, and it was under her care that he composed his greatest work, "Canticle of the Sun." After Francis's death, Clare could never be convinced to relax his strict rules of poverty, remaining the most loyal adherent of his teachings.

Though she was abbess of her own order of nuns, Clare lived as humbly as possible. She served at the table, tended the sick, and washed the feet of the lay sisters when they returned from begging. Because of the austere manner in which she lived, Clare's health suffered, and like Francis, she had the reputation for mystical powers. When she prayed, she exuded a rainbow aura and enjoyed a silent rapport with animals. While bedridden, she would embroider altar cloths for neighboring churches and her cat would bring her whatever she needed.

Even when ill, Clare remained a powerful spiritual force. In 1234, the army of Frederick II was at war with the Papal States, and the convent of Poor Clares in Assisi came under attack by a band of Saracen mercenaries. Clare rose from her sickbed and took a monstrance containing a host from the chapel. While ladders were being set up for the invaders to scale the walls, Clare calmly prayed, "Does it please Thee, O God, to deliver into the hands of these beasts the defenseless children whom I have nourished with Thy love? I beseech Thee good Lord, protect these whom now I am not able to protect." She then heard the voice of a child saying, "I will have them always in my care." In response, she turned to the terrified nuns and told them to have no fear but to trust in Jesus. In that instant, the attackers were seized with an incredible wave of dread and they fled the convent. The citizens of Assisi credit Clare with saving them from a later assault by the same army. Telling her nuns that they needed to support the city that had given them so much charity, she had them pray day and night until the attacking army inexplicably gave up and retreated.

Two days before her death at the age of fifty-nine, Pope Innocent IV approved the rule for her order, which she had formally written herself. As she lay on her deathbed, her sister Agnes and the early followers of Saint Francis were at Clare's bedside, reciting the same prayers for her as they had said for him.

✠

Saint Clare of Assisi

In art, Saint Clare is usually depicted holding the monstrance that she held in driving out the Saracens. Those working in embroidery as Clare did, frequently suffer from eye problems, and so she is their patron as well as patron to those who treat the eyes. Because gold work requires intense use of the eyes, gilders are also under her patronage. Because her name, Chiara, means clear, she is called upon for clarity of vision. Since laundresses work at dawn and her name reminds one of the effects of the rising sun, they are also under her protection. Vision and clarity accompanied Clare throughout her life. When she was too ill to attend Christmas midnight mass, she was able to visualize it on her wall, amazing those who did attend by relaying exact information of the events. Because of this miracle, she was named the patron of television, telegraph operators, and the telephone in 1958.

Prayer of Saint Clare of Assisi
Go forth in peace, for you have followed the good road.
Go forth without fear, for he who created you has made you holy,
Has always protected you, and loves you as a mother.
Blessed be you, my God, for having created me.
Amen.

✝

Saint Clare of Assisi

1195–1231

Saint Anthony of Padua
Doctor of the Church

Feast Day: June 13
Patron of: Lisbon, Portugal, Padua, amputees, barren women,
domestic animals, draftees, oppressed people, orphans, paupers, the
poor, pregnant women, prisoners, sailors
Invoked for: finding a husband, finding lost articles
Invoked against: debt, shipwreck, starvation
Symbols: baby Jesus, book of Gospels, lily

It is hard to find a Catholic church that does not have a statue of Saint Anthony of Padua. Also known as the Wonder Worker, he may be the most popular saint in the world. It was said that Saint Anthony was so infused with the Holy Spirit that he could stop the rain, raise the dead, reattach severed limbs, and have fish lift themselves from the water to listen to him. When something is lost, "Say a prayer to Saint Anthony" is a common refrain. Like other saints known for their ability to control nature, he would be seen preaching in two different places at the same time. Greatly beloved in his own lifetime, he was canonized within a year of his death, the second quickest canonization in Church history. Though he has been dead for over 750 years, his cathedral in Padua attracts millions of pilgrims every year who feel such an affinity for him that they invoke him for help in both ordinary and extraordinary matters.

A contemporary of Saint Francis of Assisi, Anthony was born Ferdinando de Bulhes in Lisbon, Portugal, to a noble family. Raised in the heart of Lisbon, he was educated at the Cathedral school. Against his family's wishes he joined the Augustinian religious order, where he immersed himself in intensive study. Finding life at the abbey in Lisbon too social and luxurious, he requested a transfer to the city of Coimbra, then the capital of the newly founded country of Portugal. For the next eight years, he read every book in the monastery's library and devoted himself to contemplative prayer.

While serving as the doorkeeper in his monastery, he befriended a group of monks who used to beg at his door. Fascinated with their dedication to simplicity and poverty, he learned that they were from the newly formed Order of Franciscans. When the remains of five Franciscan martyrs were brought back from Morocco and installed in his monastery to great public acclaim, he was

‡

Saint Anthony of Padua

inspired to become a missionary and possible martyr himself. He got permission to join the little band of Franciscans and changed his name from Ferdinando to Anthony in honor of the great fourth-century monastic, Saint Anthony of the Desert, the patron of the little church where the friars lived. Intent on preaching the gospel in Morocco, Anthony arrived there with one other friar. His plans were dashed when he was stricken with malaria. After spending the winter in bed, he attempted to return home to Portugal but his ship was blown off course and he found himself in Messina, Sicily. While there, Anthony met a group of Franciscan friars who were heading north for a gathering of all Franciscans with their founder, Francis. Anthony accompanied them to Assisi, where he attended the famous 1221 gathering of more than two thousand Franciscans to celebrate Pentecost. This brand-new religious order was fast sweeping Europe by inspiring Catholics to return to the original words of Christ. When the meeting ended and the friars were disbursing, Anthony was assigned to the hermitage of Montepaolo in Forli, Italy. Many Franciscans came from the ranks of the uneducated and Anthony never mentioned his noble background or his years of learning; he only requested to study more.

While at Forli, Anthony attended an ordination along with other Franciscans and several Dominican friars. It was discovered that no one had been appointed to preach. As his superior's polite requests for a speaker were repeatedly turned down, he turned to Anthony and ordered him to say whatever the Holy Spirit infused into him. At first shaky and shy, Anthony's speech became strong and intense. In simple words, he was able to explain the most complicated scriptural matters. His audience was astonished not only at his incredible speaking ability but also at the depth of his knowledge. This began his public career as one of the most charismatic preachers of all time.

He was sent throughout northern Italy and southern France on spiritual preaching missions. Vast crowds soon gathered to hear him. He was known

"But the apostles 'spoke as the Spirit gave them the gift of speech.' Happy the man whose words issue from the Holy Spirit and not from himself."

— Anthony of Padua

✝

Saint Anthony of Padua

as the Hammer of the Heretics for his success in winning over converts. In 1224, he received a letter from Saint Francis himself requesting that he teach theology to his fellow friars. His tenure at the college of Bologna in 1225 was followed by a move to Padua. Anthony is credited with realizing the Franciscan school of theology.

At Padua, he did much to alleviate the debt into which the common people were falling. The social economy was changing from an agrarian to a cash-based society. At Anthony's insistence, the municipality of Padua passed a law that still stands today, in favor of debtors who could not pay their debts. Debt relief and the plight of the poor in the face of increasing wealth were major topics of Anthony's speeches. It was difficult for the city of Padua to control the crowds of more than thirty thousand that would come to hear him, and he would frequently preach out in the piazzas and open fields. Luxury, avarice, and tyranny were the three vices that most troubled him. When he was asked to speak at the funeral of a moneylender he quoted the words of the Gospel, "Where thy treasure is, there is also thy heart." He then told the mourners, "That rich man is dead and buried in hell; but go to his treasures and you will find his heart." When his friends and relatives did as they were told, they found the man's still warm heart among his coins—a powerful illustration of a central tenet in his teachings.

Anthony's speaking career was cut short, however, when at only thirty-six years old, his health began to falter. An asthmatic, Anthony found great relief in rural settings among nature and he made frequent trips to meditate at Francis's hermitage at La Verna. A local count donated a woodland retreat for his use. One morning the count heard a child giggling and looked out to see Anthony surrounded in light playing with the baby Jesus. That Christ would choose to appear in this most vulnerable state to visit one of His saints is considered further proof of the goodness and kindness of Saint Anthony.

Anthony's death was the cause of intense public mourning and his swift canonization is a testament to the impact his great gifts had upon the very top of the Church hierarchy as well as the common people. He was declared a doctor of the Church because of his deep knowledge and ability to share it with others. The construction of his cathedral began immediately after his death, the people of Padua insisting that it be in the combined styles of Romanesque, Byzantine, and Arabic because Anthony is "everybody's saint." When his relics were translated thirty-two years later, his tongue was found to be perfectly preserved. It is currently on display in a reliquary at his cathedral in Padua.

‡

Saint Anthony of Padua

Though there are many older paintings depicting the many miracles of Saint Anthony, since the seventeenth century he has traditionally been depicted holding a lily and the baby Jesus. Usually there is a Psalter, or Book of Psalms, in the picture that the baby's foot rests on. This is to show that Christ comes directly out of these writings. It is also the root of Anthony's patronage of finding lost things. While at Bologna, when a departing novice borrowed this Psalter and attempted to leave the monastery with it, he was confronted by a terrifying devil brandishing an ax who chased him back to the saint. Draftees invoke Anthony for a good number on the list, and since he did so much for the poor and those in debt, he is their patron. Because he holds the baby Jesus, women having trouble conceiving request his aid. In Portugal and Brazil, his feast day is auspicious for marriages, and women seeking husbands will bury a statue of Saint Anthony until he finds one for them. They later free the saint when this is accomplished.

Prayer to Saint Anthony of Padua

Holy Saint Anthony, gentle and powerful in your help,

Your love for God and charity for His creatures,

Made you worthy, when on earth, to possess miraculous powers.

Miracles waited on your word,

Which you were always ready to request for those in trouble or anxiety.

Encouraged by this thought, I implore you to obtain for me
    [request here].

The answer to my prayer may require a miracle.

Even so, you are the saint of miracles.

Gentle and loving Saint Anthony, whose heart is ever full of human
    sympathy,

Take my petition to the Infant Savior for whom you have such a
    great love, and the gratitude of my heart will be ever yours.

Amen.

☦

Saint Anthony of Padua

R

1386–1457

Saint Rita of Cascia

Feast Day: May 22
Patron of: bad marriages, impossible causes, victims of spousal abuse, widows
Invoked against: bodily ills, loneliness, smallpox, sterility
Symbols: bees, crown of thorns, crucifix, figs, nun with cross receiving head wound, roses

Saint Rita of Cascia was the first female saint to be declared in the twentieth century. An abused wife, a mother who lost her children, a widow of a murdered husband, and finally, a nun, she experienced many states of life. Though her canonization took place five hundred years after her death, devotion to her is strong and has spread throughout the world.

102   Margarita Lotti was the answer to the prayers of a devoutly Catholic, older couple in Roccaporena, Italy. During her pregnancy, her mother had a vision of an angel telling her, "You will give birth to a daughter marked with the seal of sanctity, gifted with every virtue, a helper to the helpless and an advocate of the afflicted." Her father named the child Rita, as the angel had called her. After the baby's baptism, bees would hover about her while she slept. A symbol of divine presence, they never harmed nor woke her.

Rita came of age at the time of a deep schism in the Church–the pope had fled to Avignon, France, and the future of many religious communities was uncertain. Her true wish was to become a nun, but she obeyed her parents and married instead. The husband chosen for her, Paolo Mancini, was a good provider, but eventually revealed himself to have a violent, volatile nature. He was unfaithful, abusive, and domineering. Heavily involved in the factional infighting that gripped Italy at that time, he had many enemies and the family's home life was wrought with tension.

Throughout her marriage, Rita prayed that her husband would have a change of heart and be a better husband and father to their twin sons. Eventually, Paolo experienced a conversion when he had a vision of himself as others saw him. He begged Rita's forgiveness for the difficult life he had subjected her to and vowed to change. They had been married for eighteen years when Paolo was ambushed on his way to work and murdered, his muti-

‡

Saint Rita of Cascia

lated body dumped on the family's doorstep. Paolo and Rita's enraged teenaged sons vowed a vendetta. They scoffed at entreaties by their mother to turn the other cheek. Rita begged God to stop the boys before they also committed murder. Within that year, before they could act on their anger, both boys contracted fatal illnesses and died. Rita was distraught at the loss of her entire family, but took some comfort in the fact that her sons died in a state of grace.

With no dependents to care for, Rita devoted herself to charity and decided to pursue her early wishes of joining a convent. It is said that the local order of Augustinian nuns refused her on the grounds that she was not a virgin. A more probable reason for rejection involves politics. Several nuns came from families of Paolo's declared enemies, and they may not have wanted to

> "Here we see the frail body of a woman who was small in stature but great in holiness, who lived in humility and is now known throughout the world for her heroic Christian life as a wife, mother, widow, and nun. Deeply rooted in the love of Christ, Rita found in her faith unshakable strength to be a woman of peace in every situation."
>
> — Pope John Paul II

✝

Saint Rita of Cascia

inflame the convent with tensions from the outside world. Rita implored her patron saints, Saint John the Baptist, Saint Augustine of Hippo, and Saint Nicholas of Tolentino, for help. Three times she requested admission to the convent and three times she was denied. However, her prayers did not fall on deaf ears. Two versions of her acceptance to the convent exist, each miraculous in its own way. In one tale Rita hears a knock at her door during her prayers. Though there was no one on her doorstep, a voice called to her, "Rita! Rita! Fear not, God will admit you into the cloister as His spouse." When she resumed praying, John the Baptist appeared to her and told her to follow him to the convent of Mary Magdalene. Along the way, they were joined by saints Augustine and Nicholas of Tolentino, radiant in light. The saints blessed her at the convent door and disappeared. Rita was found the next day by the astonished nuns locked inside their convent. After she recounted the story of her providential entrance, it was decided that she should remain with them. The other tale of her acceptance explains that through prayer and meditation Rita was able to create such an atmosphere of serenity about her that it enabled her to effect a signed truce between her husband's family and the families of his enemies. Impressed by her dedication and sincerity, the prioress of the convent admitted her.

Regardless of which story is true, Rita was a dedicated nun. She tended the elderly and sick sisters and devoted much time to prayer and meditation, sleeping only two hours a night. When Rita had lived in the convent for twenty-five years, she heard a sermon on the Passion and Death of Jesus Christ that focused on the crown of thorns. While later meditating on this in her cell, she felt an intense pain in her head. A wound opened on her forehead, similar to the cuts Christ suffered on his head. Never healing, it became infected and foul smelling, eventually filling with little worms. Rita was shunned as repulsive by the rest of the nuns, and she remained isolated in her cell, praying and meditating with a mystical fervor. In 1450, the pope declared a Jubilee Year and Rita requested permission to travel to Rome with the other nuns. She was told she could not leave until her wound healed. After a day of prayer, all trace of the wound vanished and Rita made the pilgrimage. Upon walking over the convent's threshold on her return, the festering wound instantly reappeared.

The people of Cascia heard of her reputation for having powerful prayers and they sought her out to heal illnesses beyond the help of medical science. She would also mediate arguments and disagreements that seemed impossible to settle. Rita's mystical abilities became more evident while she was dying of tuberculosis. A cousin came to visit her the January before her death and asked if there was anything at all that she wanted. "Bring me a rose from my childhood garden in Roccaporena," she was told. The cousin assumed that it being winter, this request was impossible to fill. Yet there in the garden she found two roses in bloom and brought them to Rita. "Would you like anything else?" asked the cousin. Rita requested two figs from the same garden.

‡

Saint Rita of Cascia

There they were found, hanging from a tree in the dead of winter.

Upon Rita's death in May 1447, the bells of every church in the surrounding villages began to ring of their own accord. Rita's body exuded the odor of roses and her cell was filled with light. As the town gathered to pay their last respects, spontaneous healing occurred among the mourners. Many reported feeling intense joy and love, all burdens of life having been lifted. Her body was preserved and is still on view at the Sanctuary of Saint Rita in Cascia. Her feast day brings thousands of pilgrims to the town as she is still one of the most popular saints in the world. Because so many women could identify with her difficult life, her cult quickly spread throughout Europe and is particularly strong in Italy, Spain, and South America. The name Rita has become a very common girl's name in these countries.

Roses are an important part of the imagery of Saint Rita and, on her feast day, there is a procession in which roses are blessed and their petals distributed. Six centuries after her death, a swarm of bees still live in the wall of her cell. Occasionally, Rita is depicted with her twin sons, but generally, she is shown as a nun in a black habit with a crown of thorns, a crucifix, and a wound in her head.

Novena to Saint Rita

O glorious Saint Rita, your pleadings before the divine
crucifix have been known to grant favors
that many would call the impossible.
Lovely Saint Rita, so humble, so pure, so devoted in your
love for thy crucified Jesus,
Speak on my behalf for my petition which seems so impossible
from my humbled position. [Mention your request.]
Be propitious, O glorious Saint Rita, to my petition,
showing thy power with God on behalf of thy supplicant.
Be lavish to me, as thou has been in so many wonderful cases
for the greater glory of God.
I promise, dear Saint Rita, if my petition is granted, to glorify thee,
by making known thy favor, to bless and sing thy praises forever.
Relying then upon thy merits and power before the Sacred Heart
of Jesus I pray.
Amen.

☦

Saint Rita of Cascia

1412–1431

Saint Joan of Arc

Feast Day: May 30
Patron of: France, Orleans, Rouen, captives, opposition of Church authorities, radio workers, rape victims, shepherds, wireless telegraph workers, women in the military
Invoked for: strength in the face of opposition
Invoked against: fires in woodpiles
Symbols: armor, standard, sword

Saint Joan of Arc (or Jeanne d'Arc) is both a secular heroine and a Roman Catholic saint. Known as La Pucelle, or "The Maid" to her countrymen, she is credited with being the galvanizing force that returned French rule to France.

Joan of Arc was from a comfortable peasant family of five children. Already known in the village as a pious child, the adolescent Joan was at work in a garden when she heard a disembodied voice in a blaze of light. The voice gave her a simple task: Pray often and attend church. After a time this voice revealed itself to be Michael the Archangel. The angel told her that she would soon be visited by Saint Margaret of Antioch and Saint Catherine of Alexandria, two ancient martyrs whose statues were ensconced in her village church. In her later testimony, Joan said the martyrs' voices began visiting her frequently, and she was eventually allowed to gaze upon them as well. Fearing disapproval from her father, Joan never told anyone about these visits. She also vowed to retain her virginity for as long as God wanted it.

After two years, the three saints revealed Joan's true task: She was to save her country by first taking Charles, the exiled heir to the throne, into Rheims to be crowned king, and then by driving the English out of France completely. She had no idea how an ignorant peasant girl was to accomplish this. But by the time she was sixteen, the voices grew more insistent and ordered Joan to travel to the next town to see the commander of Charles's forces, Robert de Baudricourt, and tell him that she was appointed to lead the future king to his coronation.

Chaperoned by an uncle, she did as the voices instructed. The commander laughed and said, "Your father should give you a good whipping." He also ignored Joan's prediction that Orleans, the last remaining city in French hands on the Loire, would fall to the English if he did not listen to her. She

‡

Saint Joan of Arc

returned home in defeat, the voices hounding her to complete her mission. She told them, "I am a mere girl who knows not even how to ride a horse." They answered, "It is God who commands it." She secretly returned to Baudricourt, who was unnerved by the fulfillment of her prediction. Orleans was ready to fall. Desperate for any help at all, and troubled by the girl's otherworldly confidence, he recommended that the future king, known as the Dauphin, grant her an audience. Because the eleven-day journey to Chinon was through enemy territory, Joan was disguised in man's clothing.

Tales of Joan's seemingly supernatural abilities preceded her. As a test, Charles dressed a member of his entourage in royal robes while he stood among the throng of his courtiers. All were stunned when the girl walked in and immediately advanced toward the real Charles, saying, "Most illustrious Lord Dauphin, I have come and am sent in the name of God to bring aid to yourself and to the kingdom." Privately, she related to him a secret prayer he had made the previous All Saints' Day asking God to restore his kingdom if he was the true heir to the throne, and if not, to punish only him for his impudence and let his supporters live in peace. Unnerved, but not ready to accept this proof of her calling, Charles arranged for Joan to be interviewed by a group of theologians in Poitiers. They questioned her for three weeks before they granted their enthusiastic approval, amazed at how such an uneducated person could hold her own against learned scholars. They recommended that Charles recognize the girl's divine gift and grant her titular command of the army.

A small suit of armor was made for Joan, and she designed a banner for herself with the words *Jesus Maria*. Her voices told her to carry an ancient sword that would be found buried in the altar of the church of Saint Catherine-de-Fierbois. When it was easily found, Joan's reputation as a messenger from God began to spread in the general population. Allegedly this sword was used by Charles Martel in the seventh century in his defense of France against the invading Saracens. Men enlisted who would normally not be inclined to join the army. Joan insisted that all soldiers go to confession and receive communion. She banished the prostitutes who routinely followed troops. There are many written accounts of men who served with Joan of Arc

"I place trust in God, my creator, in all things; I love Him with all my heart."

— Joan of Arc

‡

Saint Joan of Arc

who declared that despite her physical beauty, they never "had the will to sin while in her company."

After unsuccessfully calling on the English to leave French soil, the military campaign to lift the siege of Orleans began on April 30. Charles's commanders considered Joan a mere mascot and thus refused to take her strategic advice. After four days of witnessing their floundering efforts, Joan charged into battle waving her banner. The vision of this fearless young girl on a mission from God turned the tide of the battle for the French army. By May 8 the English were forced to retreat and the siege of Orleans was lifted. Just as her voices had predicted, Joan endured a wound during the fighting. They also warned that she had very little time and had much to accomplish within the next year.

At her insistence, all English positions were cleared on the way to Reims. During these battles through one town and another, Joan took the lead, inspiring many common citizens to follow the troops. The English were routed completely, suffering a loss of 2,200 men, while the French army lost only three. With Joan organizing troop and artillery placement, the French army easily accomplished a feat that had seemed impossible to them–they drove the English out of Reims so that Charles VII could be crowned there, as all French kings had been before him. Joan held her banner as she stood next to Charles during his coronation on July 16, 1429. Part of her mission was complete.

Though she was in a great hurry to accomplish the rest, Charles VII became cautious and followed his adviser's recommendation to marginalize the seer. Against Joan's wishes, he signed a truce with the Burgundians, which gave the British time to regroup. He refused to support his army in an assault on Paris, a fight in which Joan was wounded and forcibly removed from the

‡

Saint Joan of Arc

battlefield. By the spring of 1430, Joan's voices told her that she would be captured before the Feast of John the Baptist. This occurred in Burgundy on May 24. At that time, it was common practice to ransom off important captives. Charles VII could have offered to pay her ransom but instead ignored her plight. The inner circle of his court was discomfited by Joan's strangeness. They convinced Charles that she had fallen out of favor with God. She was sold to the English, who imprisoned her in Rouen.

Since there were no rational explanations for her overwhelming successes, the English vowed revenge on Joan, considering her a witch with satanic powers. In order to destroy her reputation as a religious visionary sent by God, they wanted Joan tried in an Ecclesiastical court for witchcraft and heresy. Once this was proven, they could then charge that Charles VII was made king by diabolical means and reassert their claims on the French throne. Pierre Cauchon, the bishop of Beauvais, willingly adopted this plot in order to realize his own political ambitions.

Joan was illegally held in a secular prison guarded by men who repeatedly threatened her with rape. Since it was believed that a true witch was the lover of the devil, when her virginity was proven, she could not be charged with witchcraft. She was interrogated from February 21 to March 17, 1431, by a relentless panel of forty-seven judges, a majority of whom came from the pro-English University of Paris. After an attempted escape, Joan was imprisoned in a cage, chained by the neck, hands, and feet, and she was forbidden to partake of any of the sacraments. Despite their avid attempts to browbeat her and put words in her mouth, she calmly deflected the panel. These trial transcripts exist today, and are a remarkable testament to the brilliance of her simple answers. Many times, she instructed the judges to look up testimony she had previously given–exact to the day and hour. On March 1 she further

‡

Saint Joan of Arc

infuriated the court by stating that "Within seven years' space the English would have to forfeit a bigger prize than Orleans." (Within six years and eight months the English would abandon French soil entirely.)

By May, the judges had written up their verdict: Forty-two of them agreeing that if Joan did not retract her statements, she would be handed over to the civil powers to be burned at the stake. Filled with fear, Joan signed a two-line retraction. A document detailing her acts as works of the devil was substituted in the official record. Because she had done as the judges ordered, they could not execute her and the British were furious. It is not known if Joan was so afraid of the threat of rape by her guards or if the dress she had been wearing during her trial was taken away and her male costume the only thing left to her, but when she appeared before the court on May 29 dressed as a man, she was declared a relapsed heretic. Her masculine attire served as proof of her crime, and she was burned at the stake in the town square the next day. On the morning of her execution she was visited by the judges. She solemnly warned Cauchon that he would be charged by God for the responsibility of her death. She insisted her voices came from God and had not deceived her. Her last word, as she was consumed by flames, was "Jesus." In order to discourage the collection of relics, her ashes were thrown into the Seine.

A reversal of her sentence was granted by the pope in 1456, twenty-five years after her death, citing the unfairness of her judges and the fact that the court illegally denied her right to appeal to the Holy See. Joan of Arc remains one of the most illustrious historical figures in the world. Poets, painters, writers, and filmmakers have ensured her role in popular culture. While the image of her as a beautiful girl warrior is a romantic one, in fact she is the only person in written history, male or female, to command a nation's army at the age of seventeen. Mocked as a pious lunatic by many intellectuals during the Enlightenment, her reputation as a French patriot was resuscitated when she became a powerful propaganda figure during both world wars. She was finally declared a saint in 1920.

‡

Saint Joan of Arc

In art, Joan of Arc wears her suit of armor and carries her "Jesus Mary" banner. Because of her voices, she is the patron of radio and telegraph workers. She is patron of women in the military and shepherds because these were her occupations. She dressed in men's clothing to avoid the threat of rape so she is the patron of rape victims. Most important, she is the patron of the nation she saved, France.

Novena to Saint Joan of Arc

Glorious Saint Joan of Arc, filled with compassion for those who invoke you, with love for those who suffer,
heavily laden with the weight of my troubles,
I kneel at your feet and humbly beg you to take my present need under your special protection [state intention here].
Vouchsafe to recommend it to the Blessed Virgin Mary,
and lay it before the throne of Jesus.
Cease not to intercede for me until my request is granted.
Above all, obtain for me the grace to one day meet God face to face and with you and Mary and all the angels and saints praise Him through all eternity.
O most powerful Saint Joan, do not let me lose my soul,
but obtain for me the grace of winning my way to heaven,
forever and ever.
Amen.

✝

Saint Joan of Arc

1515–1582

Saint Teresa of Ávila

Also Known as Teresa of Jesus
Doctor of the Church
Founder of the Order of Discalced Carmelites

Feast Day: October 15
Patron of: Naples, Spain, Catholic writers, lace makers,
people in religious orders, Spanish military corps
Invoked against: bodily ills, fires of purgatory, headaches,
heart ailments
Symbols: book, crucifix, flaming arrow, receiving a message
from a dove

Denounced to the Inquisition, labeled a disobedient gadabout by the Papal Nuncio and a troublemaker by her superiors in the Carmelite order, Teresa of Ávila was one of the most brilliant minds of her generation. In her day, the only other woman to equal her celebrity was Elizabeth I of England, and today, the writings of Saint Teresa continue to influence scholars, political reformers, and spiritual teachers of every religion.

Born into a Spain that had only recently expulsed its Muslim and Jewish populations, Teresa de Cepeda y de Ahumada was the granddaughter of a *converso,* a Jew who had been forced to convert to Catholicism to avoid exile or death. After changing his religion, her grandfather bought himself a knighthood and moved from his native Toledo to Ávila. His son married a wealthy farmer's daughter and had nine children, the third one being Teresa. Traumatized by the humiliating treatment his family had received at the hands of the Inquisition, Teresa's father was insistent that his children devote themselves solely to serious studies. Her mother secretly loved romance novels, an addiction she passed on to her lively and charismatic daughter, and as a young child, Teresa and her brother became enamored of the equally lurid tales of the early Christian martyrs. They ran away from home, intending to go to North Africa to be sacrificed for their beliefs by the Moors. When an uncle brought them back, they changed their game to pretending they were hermits outside the city walls.

Teresa enjoyed a happy childhood until she was fourteen years old, and her mother died. After that, her father's stern hand became more obvious in her life. In order to pursue the busy social life that he frowned upon, she began sneaking out at night, frequently requiring the household staff to cover for her. She wrote in her autobiography that she often lied to her father

✝

Saint Teresa of Ávila

about her whereabouts and because he loved her so much he believed her. When it became obvious to him that his daughter cared too much for new clothes, secret romances, and flirting, he sent her away to live in an Augustinian convent as a boarder. To her surprise, after the initial shock of living away from her family, Teresa found she enjoyed convent life, which at that time had an atmosphere far less rigid than the one her father had imposed at home. After falling ill, she returned to her family to convalesce for the next eighteen months.

By the time she was twenty years old, Teresa realized that she would have to choose between marriage or becoming a nun. Many of her brothers had opted for exciting lives of adventure, becoming conquistadores in the New World. Staying home and tending a household did not present an interesting future for Teresa. When her father refused to consent to her joining a religious order, she ran away to the local Carmelite Convent of the Incarnation.

Life at the Convent of the Incarnation was far from the routine followed by the founding hermits of the original Carmelite religious order. Instead of a life of contemplation and prayer, these nuns had luxurious suites and wore perfume and jewelry. They traveled freely back and forth to their homes, had parties, and entertained liberally in the convent's parlor. Many had *devotos,* gentlemen callers who supposedly visited them in order to give spiritual advice. Since convents depended on doweries given by their postulants, those who donated more wealth held more prestige. A large portion of Spain's male population had gone to the New World to make their fortunes, leaving a generation of unmarried women behind with few other options.

Within a year of her profession, Teresa fell ill yet again and had to return home for treatment. An uncle gave her a book about spiritual exercises of the Middle Ages, Francisco de Osuna's *Third Spiritual Alphabet.* Teresa was fascinated with it and later wrote that the notion of quiet, interior prayer was a revelation to her as she suffered from constant "noise in the head" from her ever chattering thoughts. At one point during her convalescence, Teresa was declared dead and a grave was dug for her. At her father's insistence, she was not buried; instead, she woke up three days later, in a state of paralysis. She credits the intercession of Saint Joseph with her eventual cure from this illness.

It took three years for her to recover enough to return to the convent, and

"There are more tears shed over answered prayers than over unanswered prayers."

— Saint Teresa of Ávila

‡

Saint Teresa of Ávila

due to inadequate medical treatment, she never truly regained her health. Back in the convent, she allowed her spiritual exercises of mental prayer lapse. Convincing herself that since hers was an unexamined, frivolous life, she was therefore unworthy to address God with such familiarity. Passing this off as an act of humility, for eighteen years she lived a happy, social life in the convent. When her father died, his confessor warned Teresa that she was on a dangerous spiritual path and strongly advised her to return to quiet meditation. She has said that sitting quietly for one hour was virtually impossible for her. "This intellect is so wild that it doesn't seem to be anything else than a frantic madman no one can tie down." She used penitents Mary Magdalene and Saint Augustine of Hippo as her inspiration until she began to welcome these times of serenity. Gradually withdrawing from all social interaction, Teresa heard clear interior instructions and began to see visions. Her less devout friends at the convent were suspicious of her self-imposed seclusion and fits of rapture, attributing it to demonic possession. A Jesuit priest was called in to investigate these phenomena. He insisted that Teresa's visions were genuinely from God and advised her to start each day by asking God to direct her to do what was most pleasing to Him. Though such admired religious figures as the mystic Peter Alacantara and Saint Francis Borgia agreed with the holiness of Teresa's experiences, she was continually the subject of ridicule and gossip from her former friends. When she complained of this situation in one of her inner conversations with Christ, he said to her, "But Teresa, that's how I treat all of my friends." She answered tartly back, "No wonder you don't have many of them." Still, Teresa persevered in her devotions.

In 1557 she experienced her most famous rapture; an angel appeared to her with a flaming arrow and repeatedly thrust it into her heart. When he was done, "He left me on fire with a great love of God . . ." Teresa became

‡

Saint Teresa of Ávila

inflamed with a desire to truly serve God with a pure life. She decided to try and return to the original Carmelite Rule of humility, poverty, and prayer. Against incredible opposition, she began a reformed convent consisting of herself, her niece, and three other novices. Connections to the outside world were kept at a minimum, silence was maintained throughout the day, and the nuns wore habits of rough wool. Because they also wore sandals instead of shoes, they were known as the Discalced (Unshoed) Order of Carmelites.

Officials of the Carmelite Order were appalled at Teresa's radical departure from the status quo. Her fellow sisters in the Convent of the Incarnation accused Teresa of practicing a form of vanity by imposing such a strict atmosphere, and the town of Ávila, fearing this little convent without a dowry would depend on them for financial support, wanted the group expelled from their borders. But Teresa had been a nun for twenty-five years and had amassed a group of powerful allies, priests, and bishops from the Jesuit, Dominican, and Franciscan orders who helped her get permission to establish her experimental order.

Because of the wealthy admirers, the new Discalced Carmelite monastery of Saint Joseph's was allowed to remain in Ávila. Teresa lived in seclusion for five years, developing a Constitution of reforms that she felt were necessary in order to follow a truly spiritual life. Always surrounded in controversy, Teresa's confessors felt that they themselves might someday need protection against possible investigations by the Inquisition. They ordered her to write her autobiography and then keep journals on her mystical visions and interior communications. The first of these writings, *Autobiography*, was written before 1567. A copy of it was passed around among the nobility. Many wealthy women, responding to the directness and humor in its prose, as well as its honest portrayal of life in the upper classes, identified with its author

✝

Saint Teresa of Ávila

and clamored to sponsor other reformed monasteries. *The Way of Perfection,* a book Teresa wrote for her own nuns about prayer, introduced her spiritual philosophy to the outside world. When the Father General of the Carmelites inspected her experimental monastery, he so greatly admired what she had achieved that he asked her to start similar houses for men. The great Spanish Saint John of the Cross joined her in this venture.

Teresa traveled all over Spain to found more convents and monasteries, braving ice storms, searing sun, filthy inns, thieves, and her own failing health. Yet the most severe challenge to her work came from inside the Church itself. Considering the dire consequences an outspoken part-Jewish woman with mystical visions could suffer in sixteenth-century Spain, it is amazing that she never faltered in her mission. Teresa insisted that the love of God had so taken hold of her that He enabled her to continue her work as a reformer. The Discalced Carmelites were formally separated from the Calced Carmelites and given their own constitution in 1580. Her final book, *The Interior Castle,* written in 1577, is her masterpiece. Using the image of a crystal castle of transparent rooms, Teresa guides the soul inward to discover the voice of Christ.

Teresa died, exhausted, of her many ailments on October 4, 1582. Because the reform of the Gregorian calendar was enacted the next day, her official day of death became October 15.

Ecstasy of Saint Teresa

✝

Saint Teresa of Ávila

In art, Teresa is frequently shown with a book of her writings; sometimes she is communing with the dove of the Holy Spirit, signifying her divine guidance. The flaming arrow is from her rapture and, because it pierced her heart, she is the patron of heart ailments. As a writer and headache sufferer, she is invoked against headaches. In her visions she saw herself in Purgatory so she is invoked against its fires. Her nuns made lace to support their convent, so she is a patron of lace makers. Because she traveled all over Spain and gave it some of its greatest literature, she is the patron of that country. Her spirit of reform makes her the patron of the Spanish Military Corps.

Prayer to Redeem Lost Time by Saint Teresa of Ávila
O my God! Source of all mercy! I acknowledge Your sovereign
   power.
While recalling the wasted years that are past,
I believe that You, Lord, can in an instant turn this loss to gain.
Miserable as I am, yet I firmly believe that You can do all things.
Please restore to me the time lost, giving me Your grace,
Both now and in the future, that I may appear before You in
   wedding garments.
Amen.

✠

Saint Teresa of Ávila

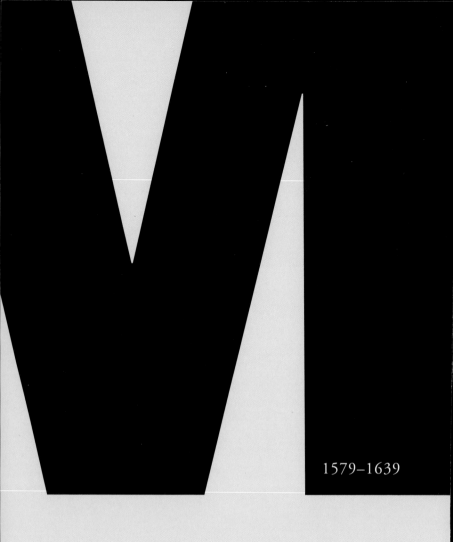

1579–1639

Saint Martin de Porres

Feast Day: November 3
Patron of: barbers, blacks, hairdressers, hoteliers, interracial justice, jurists, those of mixed races, Peru, the poor, public health, public schools, racial harmony
Invoked against: mice and rats
Symbols: broom, cat, crucifix, dog, dove

STAB. L. SALOMONE - ROMA

S. MARTIN DE PORRES O. P.

(1579-1639)

As a mixed-race man born in Peru, Saint Martin de Porres is a representative of three continents; his mother was of African descent, his father was from Spain, and he himself was born in the New World. A highly esteemed healer and friend to all living creatures, Martin is one of the most popular saints in Latin America.

124 Born in Lima, Peru, Martin was the illegitimate child of a Spanish knight and a freed black woman from Panama, whose family had been African slaves. Dark complected like his mother, he was not legally recognized by his father until he was a teenager. He and his sister shared a poor and neglected childhood, and at the age of twelve, he was apprenticed to a barber so that he might have a trade. In those days, in addition to cutting hair, barbers performed surgery, made medicines, and were much sought out for cures of every ailment.

Deeply religious, it was Martin's habit to pray as he mixed his herbal healing potions, and it was said that he healed as many with his prayers as with his herbs. He met with great success in his new profession, but in his desire to serve God with childlike humility, he routinely gave all his money to the poor. By the age of fifteen he wanted to become a foreign missionary and decided to enter the Dominican Rosary Convent as a Third Order Tertiary or Lay Brother. He chose to perform the lowliest house chores, all the while meditating on the Passion of Christ, a subject of much fascination for him. As a farm laborer and gardener, Martin developed a deep attunement to nature. Animals flocked to him and he in turn showed them a respect and kindness that bewildered his European brothers.

Since the majority of the Dominican priests were from Spain, they had little experience with people from other cultures. Believing in the superiority of

‡

Saint Martin de Porres

their own civilization, they were basically in the New World to minister to the newly arrived soldiers and merchants from their mother country. During a plague, Martin quietly taught them the true meaning of Christian charity when he volunteered to help out in the infirmary. He ceaselessly nursed African slaves, the native population, and Spanish nobility with the same grace and ardor. Because of the spectacular success of his treatments, he was installed as head of the infirmary, a job he claimed to be unworthy of. One day, when the infirmary was overcrowded with the sick, Martin was told not to admit anyone else. Yet when he found an Indian bleeding to death from a knife wound, he immediately took the man in and treated him. Martin's Superior chastised him for this open disobedience of his order, and Martin replied, "Forgive my error, and please instruct me, for I did not know that the precept of obedience took precedence over that of charity." From then on, Martin was given the liberty to follow his own decisions on treating patients. Martin proved to add such a valuable contribution to his religious community that, at the insistence of his prior, racial stipulations were abolished so that he could be made a fully professed brother in the Dominican Order.

As a priest, Martin put his missionary instincts to work, traveling through

"Compassion, my dear brother, is preferable to cleanliness. Reflect that with a little soap I can easily clean my bed covers but even with a torrent of tears I would never wash from my soul the stain that my harshness toward the unfortunate would create."

— Martin de Porres

‡

Saint Martin de Porres

the city to tend the sick of Lima. He was particularly devoted to improving the lot of the poor and the racially oppressed. Having great practical instincts, he opened hospitals and orphanages, raising money from the newly wealthy Spanish elite. Because of his ability to budget and allocate the charitable donations he was given, Martin was promoted to almoner of the monastery at a time when it was floundering for financial support. He amassed steady donations totaling two thousand dollars per week, an astounding sum at that time, to cover the monastery's operating expenses as well as to provide food for the hungry. Every day at noon he had the gates of the monastery opened so that he could distribute food to anyone who needed it. Regardless of the number of people waiting, no one was ever turned away.

His charity extended to the animal kingdom, and he inaugurated the first shelter for stray cats and dogs. It was his sincere belief that all creatures were equally loved by God so all were deserving of his compassion and servitude—even those of the lowliest order. An example of this belief was evident when the monastery became overrun by mice and rats. The prior ordered poison to be set out to end the infestation. Martin went out to the garden and softly called the rodents out of their hiding places. He reprimanded them for invading the monastery and promised to feed them every day out in the garden if they would stay away from the building. Both sides kept to this agreement, and Saint Martin is still invoked today to prevent infestations of these pests.

If Martin's great love for animals seemed inexplicable to his Spanish brethren, they grew to accept it as just another proof of his sanctity. He ceaselessly prayed and enjoyed menial tasks because they enabled him to keep his silent union with God. Martin's wisdom seemed to come from a source deep within him and was much sought after. Archbishops and students of religion came to him for spiritual guidance and direction. This was no doubt a difficult role for him, since he preferred a life of humility and anonymity. But with such mystical gifts, he could not remain overlooked. In the chapel, he would go so deeply into meditation that he would levitate off the ground. His intuitive abilities enabled him to read minds and slip through locked doors. Like other mystical saints, he was gifted with bilocation, the ability to be in two places at once, transcending all laws of time and space. Spanish traders who knew him from Lima reported meeting him in the Philippines and Japan. An African slave whom Martin treated in Peru told Martin that he was extremely happy to see him again and asked how his voyage was. When he was told by another brother that Martin had never left Lima in his life, the slave vehemently dsagreed. He insisted that Martin had come to the slaves in the hull of the boats as they were transported in irons, offering consolation and comfort.

☩

Saint Martin de Porres

By the time of his death from a high fever, Martin de Porres was a great celebrity in Lima. The poor considered him a folk hero and called him the Father of Charity, and he was honored by the upper classes for his good works and ability as a healer. His funeral was open to the entire city and was attended by noblemen, ex-slaves, and religious authorities whom he had served and advised with equal respect in life. After his death, Martin maintained the love of the Peruvian people, and his cult is particularly strong in South America.

In art, Saint Martin de Porres is depicted in a Dominican habit with a broom, little animals at his feet as a reminder of the life of humility he led, doing menial work, his love for all of God's creatures evident. The dove of the Holy Spirit is also present, stressing the divine wisdom Martin had. He carries a cross because of his devotion to Christ's Passion. Since Martin was of mixed race, he is the patron of racial harmony. Because he began his life as a barber, barbers and hairdressers claim him. He is the patron of jurists because so many important people came to him for advice.

Prayer to Saint Martin de Porres
To you Saint Martin de Porres we prayerfully lift up our hearts filled with serene confidence and devotion.
Mindful of your unbounded and helpful charity
to all levels of society and also of your meekness and humility of
    heart,
we offer our petitions to you. [state request here]
Pour out upon our families the precious gifts of your solicitous and generous intercession.
Show to the people of every race and color the paths of unity and
    of justice.
Implore from our Father in heaven the coming of His kingdom,
so that through mutual benevolence in God
men may increase the fruits of grace and merit the rewards of
    eternal life.
Amen.

✝

Saint Martin de Porres

T

1873–1897

SaintThérèse of Lisieux
*Also Known as Thérèse of the Child Jesus
and the Holy Face, the Little Flower,
Doctor of the Church*

Feast Day: October 1
Patron of: France, Russia, Vietnam, AIDS patients,
concerns of children, florists, foreign missions, pilots,
religious freedom in Russia, tuberculosis patients
Invoked for: a loving atmosphere
Symbols: crucifix, showering roses

Considered the greatest saint of modern times, Thérèse of Lisieux lived and died in obscurity. A Carmelite nun who never rose above novice, she spent her days performing routine chores and died just a few miles from where she was brought up. Hers was an interior life and she quietly developed a system of living that has since attracted hundreds of millions of devotees around the world.

Born Thérèse Martin into an upper-middle-class family in Normandy, France, she was the youngest of five sisters. The Martin family was happy and pious as both parents had wanted religious vocations before they met and married. When Thérèse was four her mother died of breast cancer and the family moved to the town of Lisieux to be near extended family. Raised by her older sisters, Thérèse was outgoing and extremely spoiled. She later admitted that she refused to do any chores, and the slightest rebuff of what she wanted would reduce her to hysterical fits and tears. When her eldest sister joined the local Carmelite convent, Thérèse, nine years old, requested to follow her. She had decided that she wanted to become a saint. The Mother Superior advised her that the earliest she could enter the convent would be at the age of sixteen. When a few months later, Thérèse fell gravely ill, her bedside was surrounded by concerned relatives. According to her later writings, she was instantly cured when she saw the statue of the Virgin Mary in her room smile at her.

The religious atmosphere of her home had been absorbed by all three of her older sisters. By the time she was fourteen years old all but one had joined the convent. Her remaining sister, Celeste, enjoyed babying Thérèse and made their father leave gifts in Thérèse's shoes for Christmas, a custom typically enjoyed by only very young French children. As Thérèse raced home from church to receive her gifts, the girls overheard their father saying how

‡

Saint Thérèse of Lisieux

glad he was that this would be the last year for something so silly. Instead of bursting into tears at this slight, Thérèse reported that her heart filled with an incredible warmth. She felt the presence of Jesus and suddenly was able to identify fully with her father's feelings. Without acknowledging that she had heard the remark, she ran and received her gifts with enthusiasm. She declared that this was the point of her "conversion." Shortly after, she decided that she too would like to become a nun. Since she was still far too young, the convent refused her. Steeling her resolve, she petitioned the bishop. When he also refused her, her father decided to take his two remaining daughters on a pilgrimage to Rome to visit the Christian sites. This was one of the happiest experiences of her short life. Together with her sister, they saw where the early martyrs died and happily touched relics of the saints. While at an audience for Pope Leo XIII, Thérèse burst out of her seat and requested permission to join the Carmelites. She was told by him that it all depended on the will of God. Upon her family's return to France, Thérèse was admitted to the Carmelite Order. Despite the fact that she was only fifteen years old, the vicar general had seen in her the resolve needed to endure such a difficult life of sacrifice.

According to Thérèse, all her romantic and pious notions of the sentimental holiness of convent life ended upon her admittance. For one thing, her beloved father had suffered a series of debilitating strokes and, because she was a cloistered nun, she could not see him. For another, her daily routine consisted of hours of prayer interspersed with menial labor. She felt her prayers were not being heard and would often fall asleep grief stricken in a state of "spiritual dryness." She also knew that the life of a cloistered nun devoted to prayer was far from the active life of a great saint or martyr; instead, she came face-to-face with her personal failings and weaknesses. Since she felt small and ineffectual as a person, she pictured herself as a tiny child being carried by Jesus. She later asked someone, "Why would I fear a God who made himself so small for me?" She discovered that if, for example,

"My vocation is love! Yes I have found my place in the Church ... in the heart of the Church, my Mother, I shall be love."

— Thérèse of Lisieux

✣

Saint Thérèse of Lisieux

she could not stand another nun, she would ask Jesus to become part of her and he would show her how to love that person. She began to apply this approach to everything in life: to food she could not stand, to chores she disliked, to being uncomfortable and cold in the convent. By accepting the reality of her own weaknesses and offering herself to God so that he could work through her, she began to see God as love personified and wrote, "It is not so essential to think much as to love much." Noting that everyone has their special talents and abilities, Thérèse decided that her special devotion would be to love. "My vocation is love! Yes I have found my place in the Church . . . in the heart of the Church, my Mother, I shall be love."

Since the Carmelites had convents all over the world, Thérèse had the dream to travel to Vietnam to be a missionary, welcoming possible martyrdom. She felt a strong desire to act as an apostle. Instead, she was diagnosed with tuberculosis and forced to remain in her convent. Her sister had been elected prioress of their house and asked Thérèse to sacrifice her desire to being a full-fledged nun in order to allay fears that the Martin sisters were taking over the convent. Thérèse never advanced above the role of novice and lacked the privileges of the other nuns. She insisted that God would not give her the desire to be a saint if it were an impossible achievement. She became obsessed with finding a way to holiness by living a small and hidden life.

By 1896 her health was deteriorating, and she was ordered by her sister to write a book of memories detailing her spiritual life. This is a common Carmelite exercise of self-examination. As she approached her own death, doubts began to plague her. She worried that there was no afterlife, that all the future held for her was a "nothingness of being." In her spiritual autobiography, *Story of a Soul*, Thérèse details overcoming this malaise with the development of her "Little Way." She realized that since great deeds were forbidden to her due to her personal circumstances, she would scatter small loving deeds, a smile or a kind thought, like flowers. By the end of her life, her devotion to love and her willingness to make small daily sacrifices had reconciled her to looking forward to her death. She knew that no act, no matter how small, was insignificant. Her wish was to spiritually come back to earth, to work without rest until the end of the world. When one of her sisters visited her on her deathbed and cried about how much she would miss her, Thérèse said, "I will spend my heaven doing good on earth. After my death, I will let fall a shower of roses."

After her death in 1897, her memoir, *Story of a Soul,* was printed and sent out among the Carmelite sisters. This story had great appeal for Catholics struggling to find holiness while living everyday lives. It became a major bestselling book all over France and has since been translated into more than sixty languages. People everywhere felt an intense connection with Thérèse. Her doubts and solution to accepting the life one is given made her a saint for modern times. Pilgrimages to Lisieux began and miraculous healings were

‡

Saint Thérèse of Lisieux

reported. During World War I it was common for French infantrymen to carry her picture in their wallets. She was canonized in 1925 and declared a Doctor of the Church for her writings in 1997. Devotion to her philosophies continues to grow. Her relics have visited the four corners of the world. Wherever they go, an outpouring of visitors numbering in the tens of millions come to be in their presence. These visits are used as opportunities to educate about the "Little Way" of Thérèse.

In art, Saint Thérèse is depicted holding a crucifix of roses, signifying grace's fall from her hands. It is said that all who invoke her know their prayers will be answered when they see roses as a sign. She is the patron of foreign missions because of her interests in being a missionary and because her relics have visited so many countries of the world. The Carmelites have had a longtime presence in Russia; their convent in Siberia has administered to exiled rulers from eastern Germany and Poland for centuries. Tensions with the Orthodox Church have made the advances of Roman Catholicism difficult there. It is thought that the Orthodox and Roman churches could be reconciled by acting on Thérèse's simple theories of divine love. Because of her dream to work in Vietnam, she is patron of that country. She is also the secondary patron of France for her writings in French and for the love her countrymen have for her. She is the patron of AIDS sufferers as well as tuberculosis, since she, like many with these diseases, have been cut off in the prime of life. Since it was her great dream to travel, she is also the patron of pilots.

Novena to Thérèse of the Child Jesus
O little Thérèse of the Child Jesus,
Please pick for me a rose from the heavenly
gardens and send it to me as a message of love.
O little flower of Jesus,
ask God today to grant favors
I now place with confidence in your hands. . .
[mention request here]
Saint Thérèse, help me to always believe as you did,
in God's great love for me,
So that I might imitate your "Little Way" each day.
Amen.

☩

Saint Thérèse of Lisieux

1891–1942

Saint Teresa Benedicta of the Cross
Also Known as Edith Stein

Feast Day: August 9
Patron of: Europe, loss of parents, martyrs,
World Youth Day
Symbols: Carmelite habit, cross, concentration
camp wire, Star of David

Edith Stein was a brilliant and well-known scholar of philosophy. A self-declared atheist, she struggled with her spiritual identity before converting to Catholicism, joining the Carmelite Order, and taking the name Teresa, Blessed of the Cross. From her isolation, she wrote meditative studies and prayed for the world. Though cloistered in the neutral country of Holland for her protection during World War II, she was not spared from the horrors of Auschwitz and died there in 1942.

Born in Breslau, Germany, on the Jewish Day of Atonement, Edith Stein was the youngest of eleven children in a traditionally Jewish family. Her father ran the family's large timber business until his sudden death when Edith was two. Her mother was forced to fend for herself and her children. She took control of the floundering company and proved herself to be a brilliant businesswoman. Though opportunities in higher education had only just opened up for women in Prussia, her mother stressed the value of higher education for all of her children, male and female alike. Edith was a child prodigy and began reading complex works of literature at age six. As a teenager, Edith renounced her Jewish faith and became an atheist. In her own words she was a "radical suffragette" passionately devoted to women's issues. She immersed herself in the study of philosophy, and, in 1913, transferred to Göttingen University where she was accepted as a student by Edmund Husserl, the philosophic genius who developed phenomenology, an early form of psychology devoted to the individual's view of reality. Husserl had a great influence on the intellectual and philosophical circles of his day and many of Germany's best young minds vied to be near him. He recognized Edith Stein's keen intelligence and appointed her as his teaching assistant. Between 1916 and 1921, Edith Stein wrote four treatises for Husserl's jour-

‡

Saint Teresa Benedicta of the Cross

nal that are still required reading for students of this philosophy, and many feel she surpassed her mentor in explaining and exploring his theories.

During the First World War, along with studying and teaching, she volunteered as a nurse in an Austrian field hospital and was confronted with the specter of young people dying and suffering on a daily basis. When a good friend–one of Husserl's assistants–was killed in the war, Edith was paralyzed with grief. Moreover, she dreaded seeing his widow as she felt incapable of offering any solace. To her amazement, it was his widow, a devout Protestant, who comforted Edith. She writes of this time as ". . . my first encounter with the Cross and the divine power it imparts to those who bear it . . ." Phenomenologists did not share the prejudice against religion that is sometimes common among scientists and intellectuals. And though Husserl himself was an agnostic, a good number of his students were adapting Christian beliefs. Edith became ever more intrigued by Christianity. While writing her dissertation, "The Problem of Empathy," Edith visited the Frankfurt cathedral. To her amazement, she saw a woman come directly from the market with her groceries and enter the church to say a brief prayer. Years later she wrote, "This was something totally new to me. In the synagogues and Protestant churches I had visited, people simply went to the services. Here, however, I saw someone coming straight from the busy marketplace into this empty church as if she were going to have an intimate conversation. It was something I never forgot."

Anticipating a day when women would be allowed to become professors, Edith earned her doctorate summa cum laude in 1917. In her pursuit of absolute objectivity of judgment she read religious tracts and wrote articles about the philosophical foundation of psychology. Though still an atheist, Edith tried doing Ignatius Loyola's Spiritual Exercises out of curiosity. To her own surprise, she found in herself a thirst for God. While vacationing with

"I had given up practicing my Jewish religion when I was a fourteen-year-old girl and did not begin to feel Jewish again until I had returned to God."

— Edith Stein

‡

Saint Teresa Benedicta of the Cross

friends–recent Protestant converts and students of Husserl's–Edith happened on the autobiography of Teresa of Ávila. She devoured it in a single night and exclaimed, "This is the truth!" She seemed to assimilate and fully identify with the inner spiritual journey of the great Spanish mystic. Since Teresa of Ávila was also Jewish, Edith felt her to be a kindred spirit. She believed that she belonged to Christ not only spiritually, but through her bloodlines as well. The study of Catholicism became her new passion, and she was baptized on January 1, 1922, with the future intention of becoming a Carmelite nun just like Teresa of Ávila. Though her mother was devastated by her daughter's decision, she retained a close relationship with her youngest child.

Her desire to live in seclusion from the world by becoming a cloistered nun was discouraged by her spiritual directors. They insisted that she employ her innate talents as a teacher and scholar. Throughout the 1920s, she worked in the Dominican Sisters' school as a German and history teacher, positions far beneath her abilities. She also ran a teacher training course at Saint Magdalen's Convent in Speyer. She was a popular speaker on women's issues and she returned to her philosophical roots by translating Thomas Aquinas and then writing a study of his central concepts using her background in phenomenolgy on which to base her thoughts. All the while, Edith kept in close contact with the Benedictine Monastery of Beuron, going there to celebrate holy days and to continue her contemplative exercises.

By 1932, laws against hiring women in academia were relaxed and Edith had assumed a lecture position at the Institute for Educational Studies at the University of Munster. When the National Socialists took over the government a year later, Edith suffered firsthand the persecution that the Jews of Germany were experiencing. New racial laws forbid the hiring of Jewish professors, and Edith's career abruptly ended. Her attempts to gain an audience with Pope Pius XI and her requests that he write an encyclical against the persecution of the Jews were never acknowledged. Despite the persecutions against her, she chose to remain in Germany, turning down an invitation to work in Argentina. She wrote, "By now it dawned on me that God had laid His hand heavily on His people, and that the destiny of these people would also be mine."

Now unemployed, Edith was accepted into the Carmelite Convent in Cologne. She went home to say good-bye to her family, attending synagogue for the holy days with her mother. She has said that knowing all her mother had been through and watching her weep in inconsolable despair due to Edith's own decision to formally enter the convent was the hardest thing she ever had to do. Edith wrote to her mother every week from the convent but never received a response. She was invested in the Carmelite order in April 1934, taking the name Teresia Benedicta a Cruce, Teresa, Blessed of the Cross. At forty-two she was almost twenty years older than the other novices. After so many worldly honors, she found doing such chores as cooking and sewing for the first time in her life "a good school for humility."

‡

Saint Teresa Benedicta of the Cross

Edith did not escape the secular world, however, instead using the time spent in isolation and prayer to intercede for the world. She particularly concentrated on the plight of the Jews in Germany. "I keep thinking of Queen Esther, who was taken away from her people precisely because God wanted her to plead with the king on behalf of her nation. I am a very poor and powerless little Esther, but the King who has chosen me is infinitely great and merciful. This is great comfort."

After her Final Profession in 1938, Edith was again researching and writing full time. Her mother had died in 1936 and one of her older sisters, Rose, had joined her in the convent. When the mass deportations of Jews began, her superiors transferred Edith and Rose to a convent in Echt, in then neutral Holland. Edith spent these years writing meditative studies on the cross and its meaning. Her last work was an essay on Saint John of the Cross, the father of the Discalced Carmelite Order. It was his words, "Henceforth, my only vocation is love," that she had quoted at her induction into the convent.

In January 1942, Holland fell under Nazi occupation and both Edith and Rose were forced to wear the Star of David on their habits. On July 26, 1942, every Catholic church in Holland read a pastoral letter from Archbishop Jong condemning the Nazi deportations of the Jews. Reprisals were immediately taken. The SS began arresting all Catholics of Jewish origin and deporting them to death camps. On August 2, two SS officers came to the convent and demanded the Stein sisters accompany them. Edith's last known words were "Come, let us go for the sake of our people." The two women were forced into cattle cars with thousands of others. It took them four days to reach their final destination, Auschwitz. They died in the gas chambers on August 9, 1942. In recent years a debate has questioned the Church's usage of "martyr" to categorize her since she was not killed for being a Christian but for being born a Jew. But since she was deported and executed as a response to the Church in Holland's stance against Nazi genocide, the term *martyr* is an apt one.

Because of her great fame as a scholar, there are numerous photographs of Edith Stein throughout her career. In art, she is depicted as a nun with the Star of David on her habit.

Prayer for the Intercession of Saint Teresa Benedicta

Lord, God of our fathers, You brought Saint Teresa Benedicta
to the fullness of the science of the cross at the hour of her
   martyrdom.
Fill us with the same knowledge, and, through her intercession,
allow us always to seek after you, the supreme truth,
and to remain faithful until death to the covenant of love
ratified in the blood of your Son for the salvation of all men and
   women.
We ask this through Christ, our Lord.
Amen.

1887–1969

Saint Pio
Padre Pio

Feast Day: September 23
Patron of: none official
Invoked for: forgiveness, healing of all kind
Symbols: crucifix, stigmata

Padre Pio was able to make people who never thought of spiritual matters, religious. He is known as the saint of the common people, always consoling, always accessible to those who visited or wrote to him. A mystic who could bilocate and read hearts, he had assured his fellow monks that he would become an even more prevalent force after his death. Today, millions of people every year flock to the little monastery in which he lived out his life in order to be in his spiritual presence.

Named for Saint Francis of Assisi, Francesco Forgione was born in Pietrelcina, a small town north of Naples. His family was devoutly Catholic, and as a child he experienced many spiritual visions of Christ and the Virgin Mary. He never mentioned these visions to anyone, because in his naïveté, he thought all people had them. He entered the novitiate of the Capuchin Friars, an austere division of the Franciscans. He took the name Pio ("Pious") and was ordained in 1910. However, he was diagnosed with a form of tuberculosis and sent back to live with his family, unable to fulfill his duties as a priest. He decided to offer himself as a conduit of suffering in exchange for the salvation of others. One day, while praying in his family's home, wounds appeared on his hands, feet, and side, similar to those inflicted on Christ. Embarrassed, he begged God to take these marks away. His prayers were answered, and Pio was conscripted into the army in 1916. While there, he fell ill with a fever that rose higher every day. It is recorded that the thermometer broke, rising to 118 degrees, far higher than what would be considered fatal. Sent home to die, Pio miraculously recovered and his father superior ordered him to the remote monastery of Our Lady of Grace in San Giovanni Rotondo, Puglia, a province of southern Italy.

While praying alone in the intense stillness of the church on September 20,

✝

Saint Pio

1918, he went into a trancelike state of "waking sleep." He saw Christ standing before him, bleeding from His wounds. Pio was intensely moved and thought his own chest would burst in sympathy, and, as he came out of this altered state, he experienced excruciating pain. He had become afflicted with the same stigmata as Christ, and a fellow brother had to lead him away and bandage him up. Though he did what he could to heal his wounds, they never closed until his death fifty years later. There are other mystical saints who have experienced the stigmata, starting with Saint Francis himself, but Padre Pio became the first ordained priest to have this condition.

Since San Giovanni Rotondo is very near the Gargano shrine to Michael the Archangel, religious pilgrims began flocking to the monastery to hear Pio say Mass. His life of constant prayer was greatly disturbed by the influx of curiosity seekers as well as those who considered him holy. However, he performed his duties so well that people could not help but be drawn to him. His mysticism extended to the confessional where penitents swore that Pio could read hearts. Many were sternly rebuked for sins that they themselves had withheld or forgotten. After going to him for confession, these same people reported feeling overwhelming joy and relief. Over his lifetime, he heard more than a million confessions and though he could be gruff and angry with penitents, he had a devout following.

Not everyone was so taken with Pio, however, and he was beset by controversy. All great mystics write about a period in their lives when they feel spiritually abandoned and God seems distant and unavailable. Saint John of the Cross has called this time in one's life "the dark night of the soul." Pio's trials began in 1920 when Pope Benedict XV opened an investigation into the causes of his stigmata. Doctors and archbishops were dispatched to interview him. Accusations of fraud and clerical misconduct would follow Padre Pio for the rest of his life as the Vatican launched more than twelve future investigations into his conduct. In 1922, under Pope Pius XI, a specialist on stigmatic causes declared Padre Pio to be a hysteric who kept his wounds open with carbolic acid. Padre Pio was ordered into seclusion and forbidden to say Mass in public. A massive demonstration of five thousand people erupted in the village when it was rumored that their beloved friar was going to be moved. The Vatican agreed to leave him in Our Lady of the Angels but issued a decree warning against devotion to the priest as Padre Pio's gifts were not to be considered of supernatural character.

While in seclusion, Pio calmly accepted his situation. He would spend hours of the day engulfed in prayer. Padre Pio has said that at this time he

"Pray, hope and don't worry."

— Padre Pio

‡

Saint Pio

realized his true vocation was to suffer for the souls in purgatory so that they might win early release. Though it deeply pained him to be under such intense suspicion, he obeyed the church authorities with humility and considered this time in his life a necessity for purging further imperfection from his soul.

He never left his monastery, yet people reported seeing him at the sickbeds of hospital patrons or comforting the fatally ill hundreds of miles away. A fellow monk wrote that he saw Pio shivering and murmuring in the middle of an intense heat wave. When he finally seemed to return to consciousness, the monk asked him where he was. "I was giving the last rites in the Alps," he was told. "It's very cold there."

In 1933 he was granted the privilege of saying Mass in public again, but only at 5:30 in the morning. The little church would be filled to overflowing at this hour; people would begin lining up in the middle of the night to attend.

Pio returned their loyalty during World War II. He promised the citizens of San Giovanni Rotondo that he would see to it that their town would be safe. The town was a target, as the Germans had stored a depot of ammunition near it. The Allied bombs inevitably missed their marks and the planes had reversed their courses by themselves. More than one officer reported seeing a monk in the sky with uplifted hands. American soldiers, hearing about this "living saint" made the difficult trip up into the mountains to see Padre Pio. They too experienced his abilities. Many thought he knew English when they went to his confessions; he was so successful at impressing his advice on their minds. On their return home, they spread his cult to every part of the United States. By 1947 Padre Pio was receiving more than two hundred letters a day requesting advice and prayers from the United States, Europe, and Australia.

Pio used his growing popularity to found the House for the Relief of Suffering in San Giovanni Rotondo. Today, this hospital for the hopelessly ill is an enormous medical complex which serves more than sixty thousand patients a year. Solely supported by charitable donations, it is one of Europe's finest hospitals. Successful though he was, doubts about Pio's real sanctity continued throughout his lifetime. Microphones were secretly planted in his confessional by Vatican investigators in attempts to find human flaws in his character.

He died in 1968, as he predicted he would. His fellow monks heard him declaring that he saw two mothers at his bedside before murmuring, "Jesus, Mary," at his death. More than a hundred thousand devotees attended his funeral. The suspicions that many in the Church held of Padre Pio were dissolved in 2002 when he was canonized by Pope John Paul II in front of half a million people. Unlike others in the church hierarchy, Pope John Paul II never doubted Pio's mystical abilities. He had been in confession with Padre

✝

Saint Pio

Pio years earlier, when he was only a seminarian. Pio predicted his rise to pope and later interceded on the behalf of a dear friend, curing her of cancer.

Today, a cathedral with a capacity of ten thousand people stands in the town where Padre Pio spent his life. San Giovanni Rotondo is second in popularity only to the shrine of Our Lady of Guadalupe. Like Saint Thérèse of Lisieux and his patron, Francis of Assisi, Padre Pio does as much after his death as he did in life to bring grace and consolation to those in need.

Because he is a contemporary saint, most images of Padre Pio are standard photographs. Because of his willingness to suffer like Christ, Padre Pio is usually depicted with a crucifix or with his stigmatized hands bandaged.

Prayer Asking the Intercession of Padre Pio
Oh Jesus, full of grace and charity, victim for sinners,
So impelled by your love of us that you willed to die on the cross,
I humbly entreat Thee to glorify in heaven and on earth,
the servant of God, Padre Pio of Pietrelcina,
Who generously participated in Your sufferings,
who loved Thee so much and who labored so faithfully
for the glory of Your heavenly Father and for the good of souls.
With confidence, I beseech Thee to grant me,
through his intercession, the grace of which I ardently desire.
Amen.

✠

Saint Pio

Written Works by the Saints

Below is a general list of works written by some of the saints we have profiled in this book. Though there are various publishers and editions for each title, we have not included these details to avoid giving preference of one version over another. Neither have we listed the many mixed compilations that include writings of these saints. Some publishers have added an editor's name or that of an essayist to the author's credit. All of these titles are available at bookstores or through online booksellers.

Saint Jude
The Epistle of Jude

Saint Benedict
The Rule of Saint Benedict

Saint Francis of Assisi
The Little Flowers of Saint Francis of Assisi
"The Canticle of the Sun" (also known as "The Canticle of the Creatures")

Saint Clare of Assisi
Early Documents of Saint Clare of Assisi
Letters of Clare of Assisi

Saint Joan of Arc
The Trial of Joan of Arc — full transcript of her trial available in book form and online

Saint Teresa of Ávila
Autobiography of Teresa of Ávila
The Way of Perfection
The Interior Castle

Saint Thérèse of Lisieux
The Story of a Soul: The Autobiography of Thérèse of Lisieux
Thoughts of Saint Thérèse: The Little Flower of Jesus, Carmelite of the Monastery of Lisieux 1873–1897

Saint Teresa Benedicta of the Cross
Finite and Eternal Being: An Attempt at an Ascent to the Meaning of Being
Philosophy of Psychology and the Humanities
On the Problem of Empathy
The Science of the Cross
The Hidden Life: Hagiographic Essays, Meditations, Spiritual Texts
Life in a Jewish Family (unfinished autobiography)

Saint Pio
The Agony of Jesus
Padre Pio's Words of Hope

✝

Canonization

While the process of declaring a saint is currently very complicated, requiring multiple forms of proof and ecclesiastical permission, early sainthood was bestowed upon anyone who was martyred or killed for their faith. The catacombs of Rome are filled with written invocations requesting those who were martyred to pray for the living. Gradually, those who lived lives of exceptional sanctity and goodness were also honored this way. In the twelfth century, the first attempts were made to unify the canonization process, and in 1634, Pope Urban VII declared that all beatifications and canonizations must go through the College of Cardinals and the pope in Rome. Briefly, these are the basic rules that are followed to this day:

1) The candidate must be deceased for five years.

2) The candidate must have a reputation for a holy and good life.

3) The local bishop appoints officials to collect data and all documentation by and about the candidate is sent to the Vatican Congregation for the Causes of Sainthood. Possible inconsistencies in stories and behavior are scrutinized and focused on.

4) In Rome, a biography is assembled. If witnesses can be called, they give personal testimony about the candidate. Eight theologians and a promoter of the faith then make a judgment.

5) If the congregation board and the pope agree, the candidate is declared "Venerable."

6) One posthumous miracle due to the candidate's intercession must occur for the candidate to be declared "Blessed." These miracles are thoroughly investigated by a scientific board appointed by the Vatican along with a board of five independent doctors. Cures must be declared instantaneous and complete.

7) A miracle due to the candidate's intercession after beatification then earns the candidate sainthood.

It is important to remember that it is God who makes saints, and He is merely using the Church's canonization process to ratify this. Though there are more than ten thousand recognized saints, those declared in the first one thousand years of Christianity were popularly accepted and did not go through any formal canonization process. It is also conceded that there are many saints among us who will never be formally presented for official canonization.

Index

148

‡

Index

‡

Index

Picture Credits

✠